THOMAS AQUINAS

The Gifts of the Spirit

THOMAS AQUINAS

The Gifts of the Spirit

selected spiritual writings
(chiefly from his biblical commentaries)

introduced and edited by
Benedict M. Ashley, O.P.

selections translated by
Matthew Rzeczkowski, O.P.

New City Press

Published in the United States by New City Press
202 Cardinal Rd., Hyde Park, NY 12538
©1995 New City Press

Cover painting by Sr. Mary Grace, O.P.

Library of Congress Cataloging-in-Publication Data:

Thomas Aquinas, Saint, 1225?-1274.
  [Selections. English. 1995]
  Thomas Aquinas—the gifts of the spirit : selected spiritual
writings / Benedict M. Ashley, ed.

  Includes bibliographical references.
  ISBN 1-56548-071-6 : $8.95
  1. Spiritual life—Catholic Church—Early works to 1800.
I. Ashley, Benedict M.   II. Title.
BX2349.T4813   1995
248.4'82—dc20   94-31599

Printed in the United States of America

Contents

Introduction

The Life of a Teacher

The greatness of Thomas Aquinas as a saint, a Doctor of the Church, and a thinker is well known. His philosophy and theology, in fact, have been commended by many popes and by Vatican II. His greatness as a guide in the spiritual life, however, is not always recognized. Yet, no author has more clearly shown that the morality of the Christian must be a life in the Holy Spirit by which we are conformed to Christ, the word of God—a spirituality of truth.

The first decisive step in his development of this spirituality was taken by Thomas when against the opposition of his noble family he chose to become a begging friar rather than abbot of Monte Cassino for which they had destined him. Thomas Aquinas was born in 1224/5, the youngest of four sons of Landulf, Count d'Aquino of Roccasecca in the Kingdom of Sicily, by his second wife Theodora. He had two half-brothers by Landulf's first wife and four sisters by Theodora. Two of his older brothers served in the armies of the German Emperor Frederick II, but his parents offered their youngest son to the Benedictines of Monte Cassino as a future monk. When he had completed his primary education the abbot sent him to the University of Naples for his liberal arts, expecting him to return to the monastery as a novice.

Thomas, however, had by then become acquainted with the mendicant orders founded by Dominic de Guzman and Francis of Assisi only a generation before. These two orders were spreading rapidly throughout Europe, attracting many young men from the universities, as well as young women from domesticity. This new form of religious life differed from monasticism, then a thousand years old, by its effort to restore the "apostolic life" of the early Church, a life of utmost simplicity and fraternity, unburdened by the complex structures and properties that the monasteries had accumulated over the years. Francis called youths to follow Jesus as the poor man, the crucified. Dominic called them to walk with Jesus the preacher searching for his lost sheep.

Why did Thomas choose Dominic's Preachers rather than Francis' Little Brothers? Thomas was a big, strapping young man but so silent that his schoolmates had nicknamed him "the Dumb Ox." Within his silence was an intense questioning—question after question that would never cease till his death. It is said that as a child he kept asking his parents, "Who is God?" Francis met the problems of his day by the example of a simplicity and humility of life which put little emphasis on academic erudition. But Dominic realized that his preachers would be of little use to the bishops if they were not prepared to confront the many difficult questions raised in those days by heretics as well as Jews and Muslims.

Consequently, from the very beginning Dominic sent some of his friars to the universities to study theology in depth and provided every priory with a teacher (the "conventual lector") to promote life-long study by all the priests. This was just what Thomas was seeking: a ministry of the Word, rooted in a spirituality of truth. Although his own brothers tried to change his mind by imprisoning him for some months, they finally had to give in to his firm determination to become a Friar Preacher.

On joining this order, Thomas was at once sent to Paris to make his year of novitiate and then enter its great center of learning, the *alma mater* of all modern universities. There he became a pupil of Albert the Great, the first major Dominican philosopher and theologian. When Albert went to Cologne to establish a new school, Thomas accompanied him and was there ordained priest in 1250/51; but soon he returned to Paris to complete his studies and begin his teaching career. During this time he wrote his first major work, a commentary on the standard theology textbook of the day, the *Sentences* of Peter Lombard.

In this work we already find that spirituality of truth which was to characterize all of Thomas' work and life. He liked to quote Ambrose, who said that "All truth is from the Holy Spirit" and himself said, "It makes no difference who said it, but whether or not what was said is true." This attitude enabled Thomas to find even in error some true insight he could use to widen and deepen his vision of God and creation. On a first reading, Aquinas' writing may seem colorless, but this is precisely because it is so transparent to the light of truth, unclouded by merely personal opinion or prejudice, open to all reality. Throughout his career he generously and patiently answered the many letters of inquiry about theological problems sent him by rulers, bishops, clergy and laypersons.

Yet, for all his serenity Thomas was not a cold intellectual. For him truth was not an abstraction, but Jesus Christ, the Son of God, present in the scriptures, the Church, and the eucharist. Indeed, the most detailed analysis of human feeling produced in the Middle Ages is to be found in Aquinas' treatise on hate, love, disgust, fear, anger, despair, hope and joy in the *Summa Theologiae* I-II. A brother Dominican who was often with Thomas at the liturgy tells us he had seen the learned master's eyes swell with tears when the beautiful Lenten antiphon "In the midst of life, death is ever present" was sung. We feel something of these deep emotions expressed in the hymns he was asked to write for the Feast of Corpus Christi.

In 1256 Thomas was made a Master of Theology (our modern doctorate) but was not immediately accepted by the Paris faculty, because a secular priest, William St. Amour, had instigated a campaign against the friars, calling them "anti-christs" imposed on the university by the popes who had wrongfully given them rights to teach and preach anywhere in the Church. Aquinas vigorously defended these rights and finally, as a result of papal action, was admitted to the university faculty. Like Francis and Dominic, who wanted their orders to serve the whole Church and not just a small territory as did monasteries, Aquinas always worked to unite the Church under the successor of Peter.

Thomas was not, however, a mere conformist but a very independent thinker. Until his time, Catholic theology and spirituality both in the Eastern and Western Church were chiefly expressed in terms of the dualistic philosophy of Plato, as it had been best formulated for Eastern Christians by the mysterious figure Dionysius the Areopagite and in the West by Augustine of Hippo. For Platonism the human person or self is the *soul alone* and the body merely its temporary garment. Such an anthropology is not easy to reconcile with the Christian doctrines of creation, incarnation and the resurrection.

In contrast to this traditional view, Albert the Great had done much to make understandable to his times the anti-Platonic philosophy of Aristotle for which the human person is a *complementary unity* of body and soul; but even Albert hesitated to abandon Platonism decisively. Hence, many of his disciples, notably the great mystic Meister Eckhart, developed a whole Pseudo-tradition of radically Platonic spirituality, today still influential. The Franciscans and most medieval theologians, however, remained loyal to Augustine's more moderate Platonism. Thomas was not satisfied with either form of Platonism. Aided by Albert's work on Aristotle, Aquinas very early made the decision to adopt the Aristotelian understanding of the human person wholeheartedly. Yet, he also strove to revise whatever of value the Church had learned from Plato so as to free it from dualism and make it consistent with Aristotle's holistic anthropology. Thus he was able to present a richer spirituality of creation, incarnation, and resurrection.

When Thomas' three-year term as Regent Master in Paris was complete he returned in 1259 to Naples to his home province of his Order. There, at the request of a former Master of the Order, St. Raymund of Penyafort, he finished his second major work, the *Summa Contra Gentiles,* to assist Dominican missionaries in Spain in their discussions with Muslims and Jews. But soon he was called to Orvieto to be theologian of the papal court from 1261 to 1264. Next he was assigned as head of studies for the province of Rome, 1265-66, and in 1267 again taught at the papal court in Viterbo. From 1259 on, he was faithfully assisted by Reginald of

Piperno, O.P., but was aided also by three or four other secretaries, to whom he often *simultaneously* dictated on different subjects!

This great power of concentration is evident in the conciseness, precision and consistency of his works, although many of them were taken down by students from his lectures. Witnesses relate that even in the presence of dignitaries at court Thomas often became so absorbed in thought that it was difficult to gain his attention. Once when he had to have an operation on his leg, he endured the intense pain by concentrating on a theological problem. This abstraction, however, was not merely scholarly, because sometimes, saying Mass, his face bathed with tears, he stood for a long time entranced. Reginald reported that once when Thomas was struggling over a hard text of the Bible, he prayed and fasted until one night Reginald heard him talking with visitors in his cell. Reginald repeatedly pressed Thomas to tell him who the visitors were, and finally Thomas made him swear not to reveal that it was Saints Peter and Paul who had explained the text to him. On another occasion he said to his students, "I have learned more from my crucifix than from my books."

A renewed attack on the mendicant orders at the University of Paris led Aquinas to return there in 1268 for his second Regency to again defend them. But now he found himself involved in another fight, one between the Faculties of Theology and of the Liberal Arts. Students of theology first had to pass through the liberal arts program based on the study of Aristotle, but an Aristotle commented by the great Muslim thinker Ibn Rushd (Averroes) that emphasized such of the Greek's theories which were irreconcilable with Christian faith. Hence, naturally enough, the Faculty of Theology had grown increasingly unfavorable to an Averroistic Aristotle against whom they had to defend to their students their own traditional Augustinianism.

First in 1270, then more effectively in 1277 after Aquinas' death, this quarrel resulted in condemnations of Averroistic Aristotelianism by Stephen Tempier, Archbishop of Paris, and at Oxford by a Dominican Archbishop, Robert Kilwardy, which also seemed to implicate Aquinas' Aristotelian views although he was not named.

Thus the final period of Aquinas' life was devoted to the mature formulation of his theology in the *Summa Theologiae* and to defending his use of Aristotle in theology by writing commentaries on Aristotle's works, many of them dealing with problems in natural science, ethics and politics. Until Thomas was canonized in 1323 his teaching remained suspect in Paris and Oxford, especially among Franciscan theologians loyal to the Platonism of Augustine. The loyalty of his Dominican disciples alone kept it alive.

Yet, Aquinas' last years at Paris (1269-72) and then at Naples (1272-73) were his most fruitful, during which, besides the major works just mentioned, he wrote extensively. He was able to get so much work done only by unremitting concentration. Rising early each day he confessed his sins to his companion Reginald of Piperno and said Mass, made his thanksgiving by serving Reginald's Mass, and then went to his classroom. After teaching the morning class he wrote or dictated to several secretaries until noon. After dinner he prayed in his cell, took a brief siesta and then wrote, dictated, and prayed until time to attend midnight Matins and only then went to bed to rise early for another day.

It was at Naples during the Lent of 1273 that Aquinas preached in the vernacular on the creed, the commandments, the Our Father, and the Hail Mary. But on December 1273 something occurred during his celebration of Mass that caused him to cease all writing and teaching. To Reginald's anxious inquiries he simply said, "I can write no more. Compared to what has now been revealed to me all I have written seems only straw." He went to see his sister, Countess Theodora, but was hardly able to speak to her and soon took to his bed. Since he had written much on the differences between the Eastern and Western Churches, Pope Gregory X sent for him to attend the Council of Lyons at which an ecumenical reunion was to be attempted. Thomas set out on the journey, hoping no doubt to meet his old teacher Albert again, who had also been summoned. As he rode along in his strange condition of mind he struck his head against a low branch, and was cared for at the home of his niece Francesca in the castle of Maenza. There he was still able to celebrate Mass, but growing worse he asked to die in the nearby Cistercian Abbey of Fossanova. On receiving viaticum in preparation for his death on March 7, 1274, he said to those at his bedside, "I have taught and written much on this most holy Body and the other sacraments, according to my faith in Christ and the holy Roman Church, to whose judgment I submit all my teaching."

Thomas was canonized in 1323 and declared a Doctor of the Church in 1567. In 1879 Leo XIII commended his teaching as the "Common Doctor of the Church" in the encyclical *Aeterni Patris*, and in 1880 made his philosophy and theology the basis of Catholic education. Vatican II said, "In order to make the mysteries of salvation known as thoroughly as possible, students [for the priesthood] should learn to penetrate them more deeply with the help of speculative reason exercised under the tutelage of St. Thomas." His spirituality is indeed an "in-depth penetration" of "the mysteries of salvation."

A Spirituality of the Love of Truth

For Aquinas God is truth, but that truth is also love and therefore above all things lovable. Because God is truth and truth breathes forth love, so from God proceeds the Word of truth and the Holy Spirit of love. For no other reason than a love that seeks to share its joy with others, God has freely created the universe in all its variety and order. The crown of creation are creatures who are persons, that is, endowed with intelligence and free will, who therefore can share in God's truth and love. The vast throng of these persons are pure spirits, the angels, but the least of them are human beings who are able to acquire knowledge only through their bodies and the material world in which they live. Yet, these human persons, just as the angels, are created in God's image, since they have the intelligence to know him and the will to love him.

Human beings were created not only naturally good, but "very good" (Gn 1:31) because, endowed with the grace of the Holy Spirit so they might transcend the limits of mere human nature, they seek intimate union with God in his inner Trinitarian life. If they had been faithful they would have reached this goal and entered into eternal life in God, but tragically they yielded to the lies of Satan and his angelic followers, created good but fallen by their own free will. Humanity joined the fallen angels in their sin of pride, their refusal to serve the truth and their deluded claim to be their own "truth."

We have, therefore, lost that heritage of grace by which God intended we should find our way to God. We have wandered away into the desert of lies and sin. Yet we still retain the image of God in which we were created, though sin has dimmed its beauty.

In his unfailing love, however, God has found a way not only to restore the creation and save humanity from pride and folly, but to make this fall an opportunity to complete his creation by a still greater gift, the gift of his Son, personally present in the universe as its head and king, Jesus Christ. To prepare his kingdom God selected the poor little nation of Israel and made the Old Covenant with it, gradually educating the people to righteousness through the law and the prophets inspired by the Holy Spirit. Although many in Israel proved faithless, the work of God was completed in a holy remnant, coming to its perfection in Mary who through faith became the Mother of Jesus, Son of God, in all things like us except sin, anointed by the Holy Spirit.

If humanity had received its Savior and his revelation of God's truth and love, the kingdom of God would have been realized, but instead they rejected him and killed him on the cross. Yet, in that very rejection it was revealed beyond doubt that God is indeed love and mercy, willing to die for us, and at the same time the malice of sin and the punishment it deserves were exposed. Thus the cross is the supreme proof that God is truth and love.

God raised Jesus from death to his right hand and in reward of his obedience sent the Holy Spirit on Mary and the disciples to create the Church, the witness on earth of the coming of God's kingdom. The Church, guided by the Holy Spirit and preserving the word of God in the Bible and Tradition, is fruitful through the sacraments, giving spiritual birth to Christians through baptism and feeding them on the very body and blood of the risen Lord in the eucharist. By these sacraments Christ continues to touch and heal us, as he healed the suffering people during his lifetime by the outpouring of his Holy Spirit.

Christians in whom the life of grace has been restored by the Holy Spirit through baptism or, if lost again through sin, through the Sacrament of Penance, are transformed by the gift of the theological virtues of faith, hope and love, which unite them directly to God in the Spirit and which heal the naturally acquired virtues of prudence, justice, courage, and moderation and elevate them by grace to the service of the theological virtues.

Moreover, these virtues take on a divine mode of action through the seven gifts of the Holy Spirit—wisdom, science, insight, counsel, piety, fortitude, fear of the Lord.

By these virtues Christians are able to struggle against the effects of sin that remain in them and to cooperate with God in his work of salvation, which above all consists in growth in love guided by that wisdom which is the folly of the cross. In this journey to God, Christians are not alone but seek to serve each other and even their enemies, and through mutual prayer seek to attain the common goal of the kingdom of God. They are guided on this journey by the teaching and governance of the hierarchy of the Church, which is preserved from error in matters of faith and morals by the Holy Spirit. Christians are guided by the law of God proclaimed by the Church, but this law no longer remains external, as it did to many in the Old Covenant, but has become the inner law of the Holy Spirit, the truth and love of God by which we have faith, hope, and love. In our faith, hope, and love the Trinity dwells within us, closer to us than we are close to ourselves. It is a union as intimate as that which will be attained in heaven, except that it remains a union in faith not in vision. Then with the kingdom of God it will be completed. This kingdom of the Trinity will include all humanity and the whole cosmos, excluding only those who in their false self-love have excluded themselves.

Since this work of salvation is a work of *grace*, we can attain union with God only by prayer which opens us up to God's grace.

Christian prayer is not simply a human activity, it is the Holy Spirit of Christ who prays in us, and we pray in and with Christ as head of the Church, so that our prayer has its value from being united to his prayer and that of all the saints. This prayer is genuine, therefore, only when it proceeds from faith, hope, and love which directly unite us to God, and it becomes perfect the more it is inspired by the Holy Spirit through his sevenfold gifts. "Mystical" prayer or contemplation is simply this prayer of faith, hope, and love perfected by the gifts of the Spirit working fully. It is also eucharistic, because Christ has empowered the Church to worship God perfectly in union with its Savior by the renewal of his great act of worship on the cross.

Christian holiness, therefore, is the perfect union with Christ in the Holy Spirit in his sacrificial act of love, directed by that holy wisdom which is faith perfected, the wisdom of the cross in which Father, Son, and Holy Spirit, one God of truth and love shine out in full splendor.

The Biblical Commentaries of Aquinas

The foregoing sketch of Aquinas' spirituality is drawn chiefly from his final and supreme work, the *Summa Theologiae*. But the *Summa* is only a systematization of Aquinas' meditations on the Bible. We have his commentaries on *Isaiah, Jeremiah, Lamentations*, and *Job* in the Old Testament and on *Matthew, John*, and the *Epistles of Saint Paul*, as well as the *Catena Aurea* or glosses on the gospels, selected from the Church Fathers, and two lectures on the praise and classification of the books of the Bible. The commentary on *Job* is a major work, but the other Old Testament commentaries are somewhat cursory. Only some of this biblical material is available in English translation, notably the commentary on *Job*, the first part of the commentary on *John*, and the commentaries on *Galatians* and *Ephesians*. Aquinas' exegesis, of course, lacks the historical-critical method and to a large extent the literary-critical method of modern biblical scholarship, and he worked largely from the Latin Vulgate.

He did bring to the text (what is not always evident in contemporary exegesis) a profound knowledge of the patristic tradition of interpretation and a precise theological vision. Hence, to illustrate Aquinas' spirituality in its biblical sources, we have chosen to translate excerpts from as yet untranslated biblical works, as well as a short selection from one of his *Disputed Questions*. These selections cannot, of course, show the full range and systematization of his spirituality, but they will, I believe, give the reader a most first-hand acquaintance with the Angelic Doctor's own inner life, as he drew his inspiration directly from the Word of God.

Benedict M. Ashley, O.P. and Matthew Rzeczkowski, O.P.

Graces for Ministry

The three principal features of Aquinas' account of the spiritual life are (a) his insistence that the Christian life depends totally on the grace of Christ to transform human nature so that we are able to participate in the communal life of the Trinity; (b) that this transformation heals human nature of the effects of sin, restoring us to our full humanity as images of God; (c) that since as humans we are social beings, and since the goal of our life is the community of the Trinity, our life of grace is through incorporation in the body of Christ, the Church, and hence is a share in its mission to bring the gospel to the world.

These fundamental themes he drew especially from Paul's *First Epistle to the Corinthians*, chapters 12 and 13, but in reverse order. We have made some omissions and paraphrases in the translation for the sake of readability and have inserted section headings. Note that the word "Latin" after a reference means the Latin text used by Aquinas; NAB means the *New American Bible* and JB means the *New Jerusalem Bible*.

Commentary on Paul's First Epistle to the Corinthians

Chapter 12
Grace and Ministry

In this chapter Paul wrote to the Corinthians to explain that the charismatic gifts which they had received were not merely for personal edification but to make them instruments of Christ for the service of the community and should not be misunderstood in a self-centered way. In Thomas' commentary we are made aware of how important this theme of service is in his spirituality as the context of any authentic personal holiness.

Our Need for God's Grace

¹Now in spiritual gifts, brothers, I do not want you to be unaware. ²You know how, when you were pagans, you were constantly attracted and led away to mute idols.

Paul in chapters 12 and 13 treats of the graces conferred by the sacraments, and first of the graces freely given for the service of others (*gratiae gratis datae*) or ministerial graces and then in chapter 13 of the graces given to sanctify oneself (*gratiae gratum faciens*) or personal graces.

In treating of the ministerial graces, Paul proceeds in two steps. First he states as a principle what he intends to do. I have just said in commenting on chapter 11:34, *The other matters I will set in order when I come* means "those things which pertain to the use of the sacraments, but some things I need to pass on to you right away." And this is also the meaning of, *Now in spiritual gifts, brothers*, that is, the gifts of the graces which are from the Holy Spirit, *I do not want you to be unaware*. For to be ignorant of benefits received is the worst kind of ingratitude, according to Seneca (*De Beneficiis*, book 3, chapter 4). And so, lest we be ungrateful to God, we should not be ignorant concerning spiritual graces (as 2:12 of this epistle says, *We have not received the spirit of the world but the Spirit that is from God, so that we may understand the things freely given us by God*, and as Isaiah 5:13a says, *Therefore my people go into exile, because they do not understand*, that is, do not understand spiritual things).

Then, after stating his intention, Paul goes on in verse 2 by first showing the necessity for spiritual graces. Since, however, the necessity for a thing is most readily recognized from its lack, he points out what lack they were suffering before they received grace and says, *You know*, as informed Christians, *how, when you were pagans*, that is, living as idolaters, you had not yet received grace by means of baptism (as Galatians 2:15 says, *For we are Jews by nature and not sinners from among the Gentiles*, and Ephesians 4:17 says, *You must no longer live as the Gentiles do, in the futility of their minds, darkened in understanding, alienated from the life of God because of their ignorance, because of their hardness of heart*), *you were constantly attracted and led away*, as if with a resolute and persistent mentality (like that described in Jeremiah 8:6b, *Everyone keeps on running his course, like a steed dashing into battle*, and in Proverbs 1:16, *For their feet run to evil, they hasten to shed blood*) *to mute idols*, meant to be adored and worshiped (as Psalm 115:5 says, *They have mouths but do not speak*).

The inability of the idols to speak is especially pointed out, because speech is a characteristic effect of knowledge. Thus, the fact that the idols are *mute* shows that they have no intelligence and consequently are in no way divine. And they went to *mute idols* as they *were constantly attracted and led away*, that is, without resisting and in three ways: first, by being enticed by the beauty of the images (as Baruch 6:3-4 says, *Now in Babylon you will see borne upon men's shoulders gods of silver and gold and wood which cast fear among the pagans. Take care that you yourselves do not imitate their alien example and stand in fear of them*); second, by command of some worldly prince (as one reads in Daniel 3:1 that Nebuchadnezzar compelled men to adore the golden statue, and also in 2

Maccabees 6:7, where it is said of some that *at the monthly celebration of the king's birthday the Jews had from bitter necessity to partake of the sacrifices*); third, by the instigation of demons, who crave above all that divine worship be shown toward them (as Matthew 4:9 says, *All these things will I give you if you will prostrate yourself and worship me*). Hence they went to worship idols as they were led away, that is, without any resistance, like the foolish young man of Proverbs 7:22: *He follows her [the prostitute] stupidly, as an ox is led to slaughter.* Thus it is clear that before humans receive grace they run to sin without offering any resistance.

Special mention is made of the sin of idolatry for three reasons. First, because it is a very grave sin to introduce another god, just as it is a very grave offense against the king to introduce another king into a kingdom (as Job 31:26 says, *Had I looked upon the sun as it shone, or the moon in the splendor of its progress, and had my heart been secretly enticed to waft them a kiss with my hand,* that is, behaved like a worshiper of the sun and the moon—which is a very great evil and a denial of the most high God). Second, because from the sin of idolatry all other sins arose (as Wisdom 14:12 says, *For the source of wantonness is the devising of idols; and their invention was a corruption of life*). Third, because this sin was common among the Gentiles they committed it without a second thought (as Psalm 96:5 says, *All the gods of the nations do nothing, but the Lord made the heavens*).

Some have claimed that although those in a state of mortal sin cannot be freed from the sin to which they are subject without some sort of grace (since according to Romans 3:24, *They are justified freely by his grace,* remission of sin does not occur without grace), nevertheless, they can preserve themselves from mortal sin by their free will without grace.

This opinion, however, does not seem to be true. First of all, because no one sins mortally except by transgressing some precept of the law, hence, no one is able to preserve himself from mortal sin unless he keeps all the precepts of the law. But if persons could preserve themselves from mortal sin simply by their free will, they could observe all the precepts of the law without grace—which is the heresy of Pelagianism. Second, because no one is able to have love, by which God is loved above all things, without grace (as Romans 5:5 says, *The love of God has been poured out in our hearts by the Holy Spirit that has been given to us*). But it is not possible for a person to avoid all sins unless he loves God above all things, since the less someone is loved the more likely that one is to be held in contempt. Hence, it is possible for someone who lacks grace to abstain from sin, but only for a certain time, since eventually he will meet some temptation for which he will hold God's law in contempt, and he will thereby be led to commit sin. And so the apostle says distinctly, *constantly attracted and led away*, that is, into temptation.

One Lord, Many Graces

After showing our total dependence on the grace of Christ, Paul emphasizes that the personal equality of all members of the Christian community is not contradictory to the diversity of gifts, since these gifts are given to serve the community. Thomas, a profound philosopher, explains this paradox of *unum in pluribus*, unity in diversity. Note that the *Gloss* frequently referred to in this commentary is the *Glossa Ordinaria*, compiled from patristic writings under the direction of Anselm of Laon (d. 1117), widely used by medieval theologians.

> [3]Therefore, I tell you that nobody speaking by the spirit of God says, "Jesus be accursed." And no one can say, "Jesus is Lord," except in the Holy Spirit. [4]There are different kinds of spiritual gifts but the same Spirit; [5]there are different forms of service but the same Lord; [6]there are different workings but the same God, who produces all of them in everyone.

Then when in verse 3a Paul says, *Therefore, I tell you that nobody speaking by the spirit of God says, "Jesus be accursed [Greek: anathema],"* he concludes his argument with two effects of grace. The first is that it enables one to abstain from sin. The second is that it enables one to do good; this he will explain in verse 3b, *And no one can say, "Jesus is Lord," except in the Holy Spirit.*

As to the first effect, therefore, he says: Because of the fact that when you were without grace you ran readily into sin, *Therefore, I tell you* that if you only had grace, this would not have happened to you, since *nobody speaking by the spirit of God*, that is, by the Holy Spirit, *says, "Jesus be accursed [anathema],"* that is, blasphemes against Jesus (as 1 John 4:3 says, *Every spirit which does not acknowledge Jesus does not belong to God*). Note that Paul mentions the most serious sin that grace can prevent, namely, blasphemy, with the implication that other less serious sins are also included.

Yet this saying *"Jesus be accursed [anathema]"* can also be understood to refer to every mortal sin. For *anathema* means "separation," since it is derived from *ana*, meaning "up," and *thesis*, meaning "put," as if to say "put up," because in ancient times objects which were taboo would be hung up in the temples or other public places. Just so, every mortal sin separates one from Jesus (as Isaiah 59:2 says, *It is your crimes that separate you from your God*). Whoever sins mortally, therefore, says, at least in his heart, *Jesus be accursed*, that is, "let me be separated from Jesus." Therefore, no one speaking in the Spirit of God can say, *Jesus be accursed*, because no one acting through the Spirit of God sins mortally (as Wisdom 1:6 says, *For wisdom is a kindly spirit, yet she acquits not the blasphemer of his guilty lips*).

It might appear from this text of Paul that whoever has the Holy Spirit is incapable of sinning mortally (as it also seems to say in 1 John 3:9, *No one who is begotten by God commits sin, because God's seed remains in him*), but it should be noted, that insofar as one acts from the Spirit of God, one does not sin but rather is restrained from sin. Nevertheless, a person can commit sin from a failure of the human will, which resists the Holy Spirit (as Stephen in Acts of the Apostles 7:51 says to those who were about to stone him, *You stiff-necked people, uncircumcised in heart and ears, you always oppose the Holy Spirit, you are just like your ancestors*), for in this present life, the indwelling of the Holy Spirit does not totally remove the capacity to sin. Hence, Paul clearly did not say, "No one *having* the Spirit of God," but rather "No one *speaking by* the Spirit of God, commits the sin of blasphemy."

Then, in verse 3b, when he says, *And no one can say "Jesus is Lord," except in the Holy Spirit*, Paul presents the second effect of grace, that is, that without grace we humans can do no good. But this seems to be contradicted by other passages of scripture because, although it is by the Holy Spirit that we are led into the kingdom of heaven (as Psalm 143:10 says, *May your kindly spirit lead me on ground that is level*), yet the Lord says in Matthew 7:21, *Not everyone who says to me, "Lord, Lord," will enter the kingdom of heaven*. Therefore, it seems not everyone who says "Jesus is Lord" says this in the Holy Spirit.

Yet, to this argument it can be responded that to say something *in the Holy Spirit* can be understood in two different senses. In one way, the Holy Spirit moves a person to speak without indwelling the person. For the Holy Spirit does move the hearts of some people to speak, even though he does not dwell in them. Thus we read in John 11:49 ff. that when Caiaphas predicted the usefulness of Christ's death, he did not speak on his own but through a spirit of prophecy. We also read in Numbers 23 and 24, that Balaam predicted many things because he was moved by the Holy Spirit, even though the Spirit did not dwell in him. Hence it should be understood that no one can say anything which is true except by being moved by the Holy Spirit; he is the Spirit of truth of whom John 16:13 says, *But when he comes, the Spirit of truth, he will guide you to all truth*. Hence, also in the *Gloss* Ambrose says with regard to this verse, "Every truth by whomever it is said is from the Holy Spirit." This is especially true of those things which are matters of faith; these are held by a special revelation of the Holy Spirit. Among these is the fact that Jesus is Lord of all (as Acts of the Apostles 2:36 says, *Let the whole house of Israel know for certain that God has made him both Lord and Messiah, this Jesus whom you crucified*). But there is another way to understand these words: Someone speaks by the Holy Spirit who is both moved by the Spirit and in whom the Spirit dwells. In such a one, it is true also that what is *said*, is expressed not only by the mouth but also in that one's heart and action. For something can be *said* in the heart (as Psalm 14:1 says, *Fools say in their hearts, "There is no God"*), and it can also be said in action, in as much as by an exterior act someone manifests what is in his mind. Hence, unless one possesses the Holy Spirit, no one can say Jesus is Lord in such a way that he not only confesses this with his mouth but also reverences him in his heart and obeys him as Lord in his actions.

Thus from what has been said, we can conclude three things about grace. The first is that without it humans cannot avoid sin (as Psalm 94:17 says, *If the Lord were not my help, I would long have been silent in the grave*). The second is that by means of grace sin can be avoided (as 1 John 3:9 says, *No one who is begotten by God commits sin*). The third is that without grace we cannot do good (as John 15:5 says, *Without me you can do nothing*).

Then when Paul says in verse 4, *There are different kinds of spiritual gifts but the same Spirit*, he begins to distinguish the different ministerial graces. First, he distinguishes them in general, then, in verse 7, he makes this clear in specific instances. Here, in verse 4, he distinguishes these graces in general.

As to what the grace of the Holy Spirit confers, three things need to be considered: first, the power of humans to act; second, the authority to act; third, how this power can be exercised with authority. A gift of grace confers a certain power, for example, the power to prophesy or to perform miracles, etc. The authority to exercise such powers comes from some office, for example, from apostleship, etc. To exercise such power authoritatively pertains to the realm of action. Therefore, Paul distinguishes first, graces; second, offices; and third, activities.

With regard to the different kinds of graces, he shows why different graces are needed. The plenitude of grace is not bestowed on everyone but only on Christ to whom the Spirit has been given without measure, *For just as the Father has life in himself, so also has he given to his Son the possession of life in himself* (Jn 5:26). But for the rest of us, there are different graces, because certain graces abound in one person and other graces in another. Just as in a natural body the head contains all the senses, but other members do not, so it is in the Church: Christ has all the graces, but among the members they are divided up. This is what Genesis 2:12 means when it speaks of the river, that is, of graces that flow out to water the Garden of Eden and are then divided into four main streams; and what Matthew 25:15 means when the parable relates that a master, going on a journey, summoned his servants and *to one he gave five talents, to another two, to another, one—to each according to his ability.*

Yet, although the gifts of grace that different people have are different, nevertheless they are not given by different givers, as the Gentiles thought when they attributed wisdom to Minerva, speech to Mercury, etc. To exclude any such misunderstanding Paul adds *but the same Spirit*, namely the Holy Spirit, who is the author of all graces (as Ephesians 4:4 says there is *one body and one Spirit*, and Wisdom 7:22 says, the Spirit, though one, is *manifold*, one in person, manifold in the graces he gives).

Paul then presents the differences among offices, when he says in verse 5, *There are different forms of service.* Different ministries and offices are needed for the governing of the Church, and these pertain to her beauty and completeness. This is typified by the orders of ministers which the queen of Sheba so admired in the house of Solomon, as we read in 1 Kings 10:5. Nevertheless, all these servants serve one Lord, and so Paul adds, *but the same Lord*, as earlier in this epistle at 8:6 he said, *For us there is one Lord, Jesus Christ, through whom all things are.*

Next, in verse 6, Paul presents the differences among activities, when he says, *There are different workings but the same God, who produces all of them in everyone*, that is, activities by which one benefits, such as services to one's neighbor (as Psalm 104:23 says, *People go forth to their work, to their labor till evening falls*), that is, the work which is proper to each (as Sirach 33:11 says, *Yet with his great knowledge the Lord made men unalike; in different paths he has them walk*, that is, gives them different work). But all these activities proceed from one source. So Paul adds, *But the same God, who produces all of them*, as the First Cause creating all actions. Yet, lest other causes should seem to be superfluous, he also adds *in every-*

one, because the First Cause is also at work in secondary causes (as John 26:12 says, *For it is you who have accomplished all we have done*). Note that the apostle very fittingly attributes all graces to the Spirit who is Love, because it is out of love that a master gives something freely to a servant who serves him. All actions pertain to God as to the First Cause who sets them in motion. Note also that where Paul says *Spirit*, this may refer to the person of the Holy Spirit; where he says *Lord*, to the person of the Son; where he says *God*, to the person of the Father. Or else all three names can be attributed to the Holy Spirit, who is the Lord God.

The Ministerial Graces

Paul elaborates on the diversity of ministries in the unity of the Church, naming gifts that in our time seem to have been renewed in the charismatic movement. A feature of Thomas' theology is his "pluralism." He took great pleasure in the diversity of created beings and how each contributes something unique to the creation, so that it can better mirror the infinite plenitude of God.

> [7]To each individual the manifestation of the Spirit is given for some benefit. [8]To one is given through the Spirit the expression of wisdom; to another the expression of knowledge according to the same Spirit; [9]to another faith by the same Spirit, to another gifts of healing by the one Spirit; [10]to another mighty deeds, to another prophecy; to another discernment of spirits; to another varieties of tongues; to another interpretation of tongues. [11]But one and the same Spirit produces all of these, distributing them individually to each person as he wishes.

Paul, in verses 5-6, has affirmed in a general way the differences among ministerial graces, offices, and actions. Now he makes this clearer by citing specific examples; first, in verses 7-27, with regard to the kinds of graces; then, in verse 28, with regard to the kinds of offices. As to the kinds of ministerial graces, in verse 7 he treats of the differences among them in particular and speaks first of their nature; then of their differences in verses 8-10; then of their actions in verse 11; and finally sums up his exposition with a simile in verse 12.

Thus, after saying in verses 5-6 that there are differences among the graces, he now says first of all in verse 7, *To each individual the manifestation of the Spirit is given* to indicate who receives these graces. Just as there is no part of the human body which does not share in some way in sensation and movement, originating in the head, so there is no one in the Church who does not share in something of the graces of the Holy Spirit (as the parable of Matthew 25:15 says, *He gave to each according to his ability,* and Ephesians 4:7 says, *Grace was given to each of us according to the measure of Christ's gift*). The phrase *the manifestation of the Spirit* points out the role of the ministerial graces.

The personal graces enable the Holy Spirit to dwell in us; the ministerial graces do not do this but only enable the Holy Spirit to be made manifest, just as the interior movement of the heart is made manifest by the voice (as John 3:8 says, *The wind blows where it will, and you can hear the sound it makes,* and Psalm 98:2 says, *The Lord has made his victory known*). The Holy Spirit is made manifest by such ministerial graces in two different ways. In one way, the Holy Spirit is shown to be dwelling in the Church, teaching and sanctifying her. For instance, a certain sinner, in whom the Holy Spirit does not dwell, is enabled to perform miracles in order to show that the faith of the Church, which he preaches, is true (as Hebrews 2:4 says, *God adds his testimony by signs, wonders, various acts of power, and distribution of the gifts of the Holy Spirit according to his will*).

The other way in which the Holy Spirit is made manifest by ministerial graces is when he does dwell in the one to whom such graces are granted (as Acts of the Apostles 6:8 narrates that Stephen, full of grace, was performing many wonders and signs, and these singled him out as being filled with the Holy Spirit). Such graces are granted only to the saints. But lest a manifestation of this sort seem vain, Paul adds *for some benefit,* that is, for the common good.

Thus Paul concludes that the reason the ministerial graces are given is either to prove that the teaching of the Church is true, so that the faithful can be strengthened and the faithless be converted; or else to manifest the sanctity of someone as an example to others. (As Paul says later in this epistle, 14:12, *Since you strive eagerly for spirits, seek to have an abundance of them for building up the Church*, and as he said of himself earlier, at 10:33, *I try to please everyone in every way, not seeking my own benefit but that of the many, that they may be saved*).

Then, when in verse 8 he says, *To one is given through the Spirit the expression of wisdom; to another the expression of knowledge according to the same Spirit*, he begins to enumerate the kinds of ministerial graces. As has been said, they are given for the common good, and so they should be classified according as each kind of grace can be used to obtain the salvation of others. Yet we cannot save another by changing the other from within—only God can do that—but only from without by persuasion. And this requires three things: first, the ability to give persuasive arguments; second, the ability to confirm these arguments; third, the ability to present these arguments in a way that the one to be persuaded can understand.

Now to be able to make a convincing argument, one must be familiar with the conclusions to be proved and be certain about the principles proper to the matter about which we are trying to be convincing. Some of the conclusions to be proved about matters of salvation are primary, and some secondary. The primary conclusions concern divine things, and these pertain to wisdom, which, as Augustine says in *De Trinitate*, book 13, is "knowledge (science) of divine things." Of such matters, Paul says in verse 8a, *To one is given through the Spirit the expression of wisdom*, that is, to be persuasive about knowledge concerning divine things. In Luke 21:15 Jesus promises, *For I myself shall give you a wisdom in speaking that all your adversaries will be powerless to resist or refute*, and earlier in this epistle, 2:6, Paul says, *We do speak wisdom to those who are mature.*

On the other hand, secondary conclusions are those which

pertain to knowledge of created beings and this knowledge is called "science," according to Augustine in the passage already cited. And in this regard, Paul adds in verse 8b, *to another the expression of knowledge according to the same Spirit*, in order that through the science of created beings one might be able to show those things that reveal the Creator. For to this "science" belongs that "by which the holy faith is defended and strengthened" but not whatever in the human sciences are mere matters of curiosity, as Augustine says in the same passage. (Wisdom 10:10 says, *She [wisdom] gave him knowledge of holy things*, and Isaiah 33:6 says, *That which makes her [Zion's] season lasting, the riches that save her, are wisdom and knowledge*). Nevertheless, it should be noted that wisdom and knowledge are counted among the seven gifts of the Holy Spirit, as listed in Isaiah 11:2. Hence, clearly, the apostle places among the ministerial graces not these gifts of wisdom and knowledge but simply an *expression* of wisdom and of knowledge. Such *expressions* enable a person to persuade others by speaking about those things which pertain to wisdom and to knowledge.

The principles of the doctrine of salvation are the articles of faith, and so Paul adds in verse 9a, *to another faith [is given] by the same Spirit*. But this *faith* is not to be understood as the theological virtue of faith, for that is common to all the members of Christ (as we read in Hebrews 11:6, *Without faith it is impossible to please God*.) It is, rather, to be understood either as the *expression* of faith, whereby a person can correctly present those things which are of the faith, or as the certitude of faith, which some have in a more excellent way (as Jesus says to the Canaanite woman in Matthew 15:28, *O woman, great is your faith!*). Such truths as pertain to saving doctrine cannot be confirmed or proved by reasoning, for they go beyond human reason (according to Sirach 3:22, *With what is too much for you meddle not, when shown things beyond human understanding*). They are confirmed or proved by some divine sign. Thus, when Moses was being sent to the people of Israel, he received a sign from God by which he could confirm those things which he said on God's behalf (as is clear from the miracle of Moses' staff, recounted in Exodus 4:1-9). This is somewhat like the way a royal seal confirms that something is a matter of the king's command.

One way something is taken as a sign from God is that only God can do it. Miracles are this sort of sign, and Paul here distinguishes two types of miracles. First he says in verse 9b, *to another [are given] gifts of healing by the one Spirit* (as Jeremiah 17:14 says, *Heal me, Lord, that I may be healed*). By signs of this sort one is persuaded not only by the magnitude of the deed but also by its beneficence. But then Paul says in verse 10a, *to another [are given] mighty deeds*, by which one is persuaded solely because of the greatness of the deed—for instance, when the sea is divided (as we read in Exodus 14:21) or the sun and the moon stand still in the sky (as we read in Joshua 10:13). Galatians 3:5 speaks of the *One who supplies the Spirit to you and works mighty deeds among you.*

Another way that something is taken as a divine sign is that only God can know about it, for example, foreknowledge of future events. In Isaiah 41:22-23 God challenges the false prophets, *Let them come forward and foretell to us what it is that shall happen! . . . Foretell the things that shall come afterward, that we know that you are gods!* And in this regard Paul says in verse 10b, *to another [is given] prophecy*, which is a divine revelation, announcing future events with unshakable truth. Joel 3:1 says, *I will pour out my spirit upon all mankind. Your sons and daughters shall prophesy.* And another example is knowledge of the human heart (as Jeremiah 17:9-10 says, *More tortuous than all else is the human heart, beyond all remedy, who can understand it? I, the Lord, alone probe the mind and test the heart*). Hence, Paul adds in verse 10c, *to another [is given the] discernment of spirits*, by which gift a person can know by what spirit another is moved to speak or to act—for instance, by a spirit of love or by a spirit of envy (as 1 John 4:1 says, *Do not trust every spirit, but test the spirits to see whether they belong to God*).

The ability to speak persuasively consists also in being able to speak in a way others can understand. This can be impeded in two ways. One way is by the diversity of languages. But there is a remedy for this: Paul says in verse 10d, *to another [is given] a variety of tongues* [Latin: *linguarum*], by which gift a person can speak in different languages so as to be understood by all (as in Acts of the Apostles 2:4 we read that the apostles were speaking in various tongues).

A second way understanding is impeded is by the obscurity of the scripture passages which are cited in confirmation. Paul adds in verse 10e the remedy for this impediment: *to another [is given] the interpretation of tongues* [Latin: *sermonum*, sayings], that is, of difficult passages of scripture (as in Daniel 5:16, King Belshazzar says to Daniel, *I have heard that you can interpret dreams and solve difficulties*, and in Genesis 41:16 Joseph says to the Pharaoh who asks him to interpret his dreams, *It is not I . . . but God who will give Pharaoh the right answer*).

Next, when Paul says in verse 11, *But one and the same Spirit produces all of these, distributing them individually to each person as he wishes*, he establishes who the author of the aforesaid graces is. He thereby excludes three errors. First there is the error of the Gentiles who attributed different gifts to different gods. Against this error he says in verse 11a, *But one and the same Spirit produces all of these* (for as Ephesians 4:4 says, there is but *one body and one Spirit*). Second, there is the error of those who attributed to God only a kind of general providence and asserted that the differences between particular things come about only through secondary causes. Against this Paul adds in verse 11b, *distributing them individually to each person as he wishes* (as Sirach 33:11 says, *Yet with his great knowledge the Lord made men unalike*). Third, in verse 11c by the phrase *as he wishes*, Paul excludes the error of those who attributed the diversity of graces either to fate or to human merit and not solely to the divine will. Such were the Macedonians,* who said that the Holy Spirit is simply the action of the Father and the Son. In John 3:8 we read that *the wind blows where it wills . . . so it is with everyone who is born of the Spirit*, that is, that the Holy Spirit is a divine Person.

---

* Followers of the fourth-century heretic Macedonius.

The Church, Christ's Mystical Body

Thomas was deeply convinced of Paul's teaching that by grace we are truly incorporated in Christ as his body, the Church, and only as part of this graced community can we journey to God.

> [12]As a body is one though it has many parts, and all the parts of the body, though many, are one body, so also Christ. [13]For in one Spirit we were all baptized into one body, whether Jews or Greeks, slaves or free persons, and we all were given to drink of one Spirit. [14]Now the body is not a single part, but many.

After he has shown how the ministerial graces differ, Paul now makes this clear by the simile of a natural body. In verse 12 he first presents this simile in general terms, then applies it in verse 13, and in verses 14-31 shows how it is exemplified.

To begin with, consider that according to Aristotle's *Metaphysics V*, something is said to be essentially a unity in one of three ways. The first way is by indivisibility, like a unit or a point. This mode of unity totally excludes multiplicity, since a point is neither actually or potentially divisible. Another way something is said to be one is by continuity, like a line or a surface, which are not actually many but are potentially divisible into many parts. A third way is by integrity, and this excludes neither actual nor potential multiplicity.

Thus a house is one, even though it is built of different parts of stone and wood, which are actually united, but each retains its own function. In this third way of integrity the body of a human being or of any animal is one. It is complete when it is made up of different members, which act as different instruments of the soul. So also the soul is said to be the form of an organic body, that is, of a body that is made up of different organs.

Hence, Paul asserts in verse 12a, first of all, that the unity of the body does not exclude its having a multiplicity of members. He says, *As a body is one though it has many parts,* just as he says in

Romans 12:4, *In one body but many parts.* He likewise asserts that
a multiplicity of members does not rule out the unity of the body,
so he adds in verse 12b, *And all the parts of the body, though many,*
nevertheless, *are one body,* which is integrated from them all (as Job
10:11 says, *With skin and flesh you clothed me; with bones and sinews
you knit me together).*

Then when Paul says in verse 12c, *so also Christ,* he applies the
simile by first saying that as the human body is one so is Christ. In
this same epistle, 8:6, he has written, *For us there is one God, the
Father, from whom all things are and for whom we exist, and one Lord,
Jesus Christ, through whom all things were made and through whom
we exist.* Yet, this Christ has many different members, namely, all
the faithful, since according to Romans 12:5, *We, though many, are
one body in Christ and individually parts of one another.*

Next, Paul gives the rationale for this application by presenting
a twofold reason why the comparison is apt, namely, that it shows
how both the body and the Church are one but have many members. The principle for the unity of both is that the soul unifies the
body and the Holy Spirit unifies the Church, for Ephesians 4:4 says,
there is *one body and one Spirit.*

Now by virtue of the Holy Spirit we members of the Church
receive a twofold benefit. First of all we are reborn through him (as
John 3:5 says, *No one can enter the kingdom of God without being
born of water and Spirit*). Hence, Paul says in verse 13a, *For in one
Spirit,* that is, by virtue of the one Holy Spirit, *we were all,* who are
members of Christ, *baptized into one body,* that is, into the unity of
the Church, which is the body of Christ (similarly Ephesians 1:22-
23 says, *He . . . gave him as head over all things to the Church, which
is his body,* and Galatians 3:27 says, *All of you who were baptized into
Christ have clothed yourselves with Christ*).

Second, through the Holy Spirit we are restored to wholeness,
and so Paul adds in verse 13c, *and we were all given to drink of one
Spirit,* that is, by virtue of the Holy Spirit. There are two ways in
which this *drink* can be understood. The first is as the internal
refreshment which the Holy Spirit provides to the human heart,
quenching the thirst that comes from carnal desires and cravings

(as Sirach 15:3 says, *She [wisdom, will] nourish him with the bread of understanding, and give him the water of learning to drink,* and John 7:38 says, *Rivers of living water will flow from within him*). Another way that *drink* can be understood is as the eucharistic cup, which is made holy by the Spirit (as 10:4 of this same epistle says, *All drank the same spiritual drink*).

After explaining the principle by which both the human body and the Church are one, Paul next gives two reasons why they are many. Hence he says in verse 13b that the Church is many; first, because it includes persons of different religious origin, *whether Jews or Greeks*; and second, because it also includes members of different social status, *slaves or free persons*. But no diversity of either sort impedes the unity of the body of Christ, for Galatians 3:28 says, *There is neither Jew nor Greek; there is neither slave nor free person; there is not male and female; for you are all one in Christ Jesus.*

Then, when Paul says in verse 14, *Now the body is not a single part, but many,* he explains the simile in detail by describing the integrity of the natural body and its members, with examples in verses 15-16 and counter-examples in verses 17-20. Then he shows in verses 21-26 how the members are closely interrelated. Finally, in verse 27 he applies this simile to Christ.

Since Paul has already said that we have all been baptized into a mystical body analogous to a natural body, to describe the integrity of the body he says in verse 14, *Now the body,* that is, a natural human body *is not a single part, but many* parts, since it is not complete with only one part. Rather, it is made complete by its many parts, which are needed to serve the different powers and activities of the soul. Thus Paul says in Romans 12:4, *For as in one body we have many parts, and all the parts do not have the same function, so we though many are one body in Christ.* In the following section, Paul clarifies what he has said by giving examples from certain body parts, beginning with the parts which serve movement.

Many Christians, One Church

Thomas would have been astonished at the notion, popular today, that "hierarchy" (a sacred order) in the Church violates Christian equality. For Aquinas the sacred order within the Trinity harmonizes perfectly with the absolute equality of the Divine Persons, in fact, is its explanation, since it is the *total* donation of the divine life by the Father to the Son and Holy Spirit and by the Son to the Holy Spirit, that is, the source of the equality of the Persons. All creation is necessarily hierarchical, because without order unity and true community are impossible. It is Satan's demand for absolute individual autonomy which has almost returned creation to chaos. Hierarchical order is not for the sake of domination but of service, that is, of giving.

> [15]If a foot should say, "Because I am not a hand I do not belong to the body," it does not for this reason belong any less to the body. [16]Or if an ear should say, "Because I am not an eye I do not belong to the body," it does not for this reason belong any less to the body. [17]If the whole body were an eye, where would the hearing be? If the whole body were hearing, where would the sense of smell be? [18]But as it is, God placed the parts, each one of them, in the body as he intended. [19]If they were all one part, where would the body be? [20]But as it is, there are many parts, yet one body.

When in verse 15 Paul says, *If a foot should say, "Because I am not a hand I do not belong to the body," it does not for this reason belong any less to the body,* he mentions two body parts: first, the foot, a less noble member (since it treads the ground and carries the weight of the whole body); and second, the hand, a more noble member, since it is the "organ of organs." It is as if he were to say: "The complete perfection of a body does not consist in one part, however noble; for its perfection the body also needs the less noble parts." The parts of the body which serve its movement signify those persons in the Church who are dedicated to the active life. The feet are like the laity in the Church (as Ezekiel 1:7 says of the living creatures he saw in his vision, *Their feet were straight*, that is,

strong, firm *feet*). But the hands signify the clergy through whom
the other parts of the Church are set in order (as Song of Songs 5:14
says of the Risen Christ, *His hands are golden chains set with precious
jewels*). But the Church needs not only hands (clergy) but also feet
(laity) (as Proverbs 14:28 says, *In many subjects lies the glory of the
king, but if his people are few, it is the prince's ruin*).

Next, in verse 16 Paul gives examples from those body parts
which serve the power to know: the eye which serves sight and the
ear which serves hearing, since these are the two senses which
especially contribute to human wisdom. Sight is related to discov-
ery in it that gives us more detailed information on the difference
among things; hearing is related to learning, which takes place
through the spoken word. But of these two senses, sight is more
noble than hearing, because it is more spiritual and gives us more
precise information. Hence, the eye is more noble than the ear.
Thus, Paul says in verse 16, *Or if an ear*, which is a less noble body
part, *should say: "Because I am not an eye,"* which is a more noble
member, *"I do not belong to the body,"* it does not for this reason
belong any less to the body.

The parts of the body that serve the power to know stand for
those persons in the Church who pursue the contemplative life.
Among these, teachers, who investigate the truth on their own, are
like the eyes (as Song of Songs 5:12 says of the Risen Christ, *His
eyes are like doves beside running waters*). But disciples, who obtain
the truth by listening to the teachers, are like the ears (as Jesus says
in Matthew 11:15, *Whoever has ears ought to hear*). For the Church
needs not only teachers but also disciples (as Job 29:11 says, *Whoever heard of me blessed me* [Latin: *Whoever heard me blessed me*]).

Then, when Paul says in verse 17, *If the whole body were an eye,
where would the hearing be? If the whole body were hearing, where
would the sense of smell be?* he proves his point by showing in two
ways how unreasonable it would be if there were not many differentiated body parts. The first of these ways (verse 17) is to take
away parts which are necessary for the body; the second (verse 19)
is to take away the body's unity.

With regard to the first incongruity, Paul makes two observations. He begins by showing that an incongruity would follow, when in verse 17 he says, *If the whole body were an eye,* which is a more noble member, *where would the hearing be?* that is, the organ of hearing. It is as if to say: "If everyone in the Church were teachers, where would the students be?" (as James 3:1 says, *Not many of you should become teachers*). And again, *If the whole body were hearing,* that is, an ear, *where would the sense of smell,* that is, the nose, *be?* In terms of the Church, this can be understood to refer to those who might not be capable of words of wisdom and yet perceive indications of them from afar as, so to speak, a fragrance (as Song of Songs 1:3 says, *Your name spoken is a spreading perfume. . . . We will follow you eagerly!*).

As a second observation, Paul affirms a contrary proposition to be true, namely, that neither sight nor hearing should be absent from the body, when he says in verse 18, *But as it is, God placed the parts, each one of them, in the body as he intended,* that is, God has differentiated the body parts in an orderly fashion. Even if the differentiation of members is a work of nature, nevertheless, nature does this as an instrument of divine providence. And so Paul assigns the first cause of the ordering of the members, when he says, *God placed the parts, each one of them , in the body,* as if to say: "God has not placed different members in the body so that each of them might exist autonomously on its own but rather so that they might all come together to form one body." And Paul adds, *as he intended,* because the divine will is the First Cause of the arrangement of all creation (as Psalm 115:3 says, *Whatever God wills is done*). In the Church, too, God has arranged for different offices and different states according to his will (as Ephesians 1:11 says, *In him we were also chosen, destined in accord with the purpose of the One who accomplishes all things according to the intention of his will*).

Then, in verse 19 Paul deals with the other incongruity, when he says, *If they were all one part, where would the body be?* that is, where would the body be one whole?—as if to say, it would not exist as one body. Thus, if everyone in the Church were of one condition and status, the Church would lose the perfection and beauty which is described in Psalm 45:10, *A princess arrayed in*

Ophir's gold [Latin: *in variety*] *comes to stand at your right hand.* Next, in verse 20 Paul affirms the contrary proposition to be true when he says, *But as it is, there are many parts, yet one body,* which is organically composed of them all. Thus the Church is made up of different offices (Song of Songs 6:10 describes the queen as *awe-inspiring as bannered troops*).

The Church as Community

For Paul and Thomas Aquinas the answer to abuse of power and authority is not to abolish them, since they are gifts of God for the good of the community, but to seek their transformation by the grace of Christ who came "not to be served, but to serve."

[21]The eye cannot say to the hand, "I do not need you," nor again the head to the feet, "I do not need you." [22]Indeed, the parts of the body that seem to be weaker are all the more necessary, [23]and those parts of the body that we consider less honorable we surround with greater honor, and our less presentable parts are treated with greater propriety, [24]whereas our more presentable parts do not need this. But God has so constructed the body as to give greater honor to a part that is without it, [25]so that there may be no division in the body, but that the parts may have the same concern for one another. [26]If one part suffers, all the parts suffer with it; if one part is honored, all the parts share its joy.

Then, when in verse 21 Paul says, *The eye cannot say to the hand, "I do not need you," nor again the head to the feet, "I do not need you,"* he compares the body parts with one another to show how closely they are interrelated, by asserting in verse 21 that all the members of the body are necessary, even though some are less presentable. Then, in verse 22, he compares them as to how necessary they are to the body; in verses 23-25a, as to how much care is given them; and in verse 25b, as to how mutual is their care.

Therefore Paul shows in verse 21 how members are necessary to the body for different reasons, chiefly two. The first reason applies to parts that serve the movement of the body, and he says in verse 21a, *The eye*, which serves knowledge and signifies contemplative persons, *cannot say to the hand*, which serves movement and symbolizes the active life in the Church, *"I do not need you,"* for contemplatives need to be sustained by the work of active persons (Luke 10:39-41 says that, while Mary was sitting at the feet of the Lord, listening to his words, Martha was kept busy with frequent acts of service).

Next, in verse 21b, Paul makes the same point as regards the difference between the clergy in the Church, who are here symbolized by the *head*, and the laity, who are symbolized by the *feet*.* He continues, *Nor again can the head*, that is, someone who is in authority in the Church, *say to the feet*, that is, those he leads, *"I do not need you."* (While it is true that in 1 Samuel 5:17 Samuel says to Saul, *"Though little in your own esteem, are you not leader* [Latin: *head*] *of the tribes of Israel? The Lord anointed you king of Israel and sent you on a mission*, yet, as we have already noted, Proverbs 14:28 also says, *In many subjects lies the glory of the king, but if his people are few, it is the prince's ruin*).

Then, when in verse 22 Paul says, *Indeed, the parts of the body that seem to be weaker are all the more necessary*, he compares the various parts with one another as to their necessity. Body parts which seem to be weaker, such as the internal organs, are in fact more necessary. So is it also in the Church: The present life cannot be lived without the service of certain common folk, such as farm workers and the like, but it can be lived without certain more exalted persons, who are engaged in contemplation and wisdom, although the latter do serve the Church by making her more excellent and beautiful. For some things are said to be necessary insofar as useful for some end; while the things which are most

---

*   The fact that Aquinas, commenting above on verse 15, compares laity and clergy to feet and hands, not feet and head, shows that these are simple metaphors, not an allegory with a fixed meaning.

noble are such not because they are useful but because they are desirable as ends in themselves (as Job 31:39 says, *If I have eaten the fruits of the earth without paying for them and have afflicted the soul of its farmers, then may my wife grind for another and may others cohabit with her!*).

In verse 23 Paul compares the body parts with regard to external care. First, he presents the difference of care which is paid to different members; then, in verse 24, he assigns the reason for the difference.

Now, the external care which is shown to parts of the body is related to two things: to honor, for example, those things which are used for adornment, such as necklaces and earrings; and to propriety, for example, those things which are used for clothing, such as pants, etc. And so with regard to the first kind of care, he says in verse 23a, *And those parts of the body that we consider less honorable we surround with greater honor*, that is, with greater adornment (for example, in some places earrings are attached to the ears, but nothing is put on the eyes). Colorful and ornamented shoes are put on the feet (as Song of Songs 7:1 says, *How beautiful are your feet in sandals, O prince's daughter*), but the hands may be left bare. Similarly in the Church: Consolations should be given to those who are more imperfect, rather than to more perfect persons who do not need them (as Isaiah 40:11 says, *In his arms he gathers the lambs, carrying them in his bosom and leading the ewes with care*, and 1 Peter 3:7 says, *Likewise, you husbands should live with your wives in understanding, showing honor to the more vulnerable female sex, since we are joint heirs of the gift of life*).

Paul then continues with the concern for propriety, as he says in verse 23b, *And our less presentable parts are treated with greater propriety*, that is, are clothed by human care. Certain bodily members, even of the saints, are said to be unbecoming, not because of some ugliness or personal sin, but because of the rebellious impulses of the genitals that have resulted from original sin, or also because they are assigned an ignoble function. Thus all the organs which serve the body by excreting its wastes are treated with greater propriety in that they are more carefully covered, while the members assigned to more noble functions do not need any covering.

Hence, in verse 24 Paul adds, *Whereas our more presentable parts do not need this*, that is, external propriety. Thus, the face is ordinarily not veiled. Similarly in the Church: While those who are somehow blameworthy are to be admonished and supervised (as Sirach 42:11 says, *Keep watch over a sensual daughter*, and Galatians 6:1 says, *Even if a person is caught in some transgression, you who are spiritual should correct him in a gentle spirit, looking to yourself, so that you may not be tempted*), those who are free from fault do not need such supervision. Note that Paul observes three kinds of defect among the bodily members: indecency, lowliness, and weakness. Among the members of the Church, indecency pertains to guilt, lowliness to a menial status, and weakness to mere imperfection.

Then, in verse 24b, Paul points out the reasons for the care just mentioned. First he assigns the first efficient cause of this concern: Although human beings do in fact conduct themselves in this way in caring for their bodily members, they do so because God established this order and says, *But God has so constructed the body as to give greater honor to a part that is without it.* For human beings act this way out of a kind of divine instinct (as Job 33:16 says, *It is then he opens the ears of men and as a warning to them, terrifies them*).

In verse 25a Paul then states the final cause or purpose for this care of the body when he says, *So that there may be no division in the body*, that is, disease or death, *but that the parts may have the same concern for one another* in the body. Indeed, if a serious defect in the bodily members is not remedied, the body dies. Similarly, as regards the members of the mystical body, it is clear that a fatal schism of this sort is avoided as long as the peace of the Church is maintained by allotting to each individual what they need (as was said earlier in this epistle, 1:10, *I urge you, brothers, in the name of our Lord Jesus Christ, that all of you agree in what you say, and that there be no divisions among you, but that you be united in the same mind and in the same purpose*). In the case of the members of a natural body, there would be a division or death in the body if the proper relationship among the members were taken away.

When Paul says in verse 25b, *But that the parts may have the same concern for one another*, he compares the members with each other as to their mutual care. First, in verse 26, he describes this care: Not only do these members affect one another, they are mutually concerned about the same thing, which is conserving the body's unity. This can be clearly seen in the case of the natural body, for every member has a certain natural tendency to help the other members. So it is that persons naturally position their hands to protect their other members from blows. Similarly, the different members of the Church exercise care for one another (as Sirach 17:12 says, *Each of them he [God] has given precepts about his fellow men*, and Galatians 6:2 says, *Bear one another's burdens, and so you will fulfill the law of Christ*).

Paul next describes this care more specifically, first of all with regard to evils, where it is more evident, and so he says in verse 26a, *If one part suffers* evil, *all the parts suffer with it*. This is certainly evident in the case of a natural organism; when one part is sick, it is as if the whole body is sick, and the vital spirits and humors flow together to the location of the sickness to heal it. And so it should also be among Christ's faithful, so that each one has compassion on the troubles of the others (as Job 30:25 says, *Have I not wept for the hardships of others, was not my soul grieved for the destitute?*). Then, with regard to good things, Paul adds, *If one part is honored*, that is, in some way strengthened, *all the parts share its joy*. This is also obvious in a natural organism: The vigor of one part invigorates the other parts. So it should also be among the members of the Church, so that each one rejoices over the good things the others have (as Philippians 2:17 says, *I rejoice and share my joy with all of you*, and Romans 12:5 says, *Rejoice with those who rejoice, and weep with those who weep*).

The Better Gifts

For Thomas, the apostolic office was the greatest of ministerial charisms, because to it was principally entrusted by Christ the handing on of the gospel and preservation of the unity of the Christian community, although these tasks are also shared by all Christians. Yet, the apostolic office is only a means, not the end of the Church, which is the union of its members in the holiness of the Spirit. A sound Christian spirituality, therefore, seeks always the better gifts of holiness, not privilege or power.

[27]Now you are Christ's body, and individually parts of it. [28]Some people God has designated in the Church to be, first, apostles; second, prophets; third, teachers; then, doers of mighty deeds; then gifts of healing, assistance, administration, and varieties of tongues. [29]Are all apostles? Are all prophets? Are all teachers? Do all work mighty deeds? [30]Do all have gifts of healing? Do all speak in tongues? Do all interpret? [31]Strive eagerly for the greatest spiritual gifts. But I shall show you a still more excellent way.

As promised, in verse 27 Paul applies the analogy of the human body to the Church, first of all with regard to the unity of body, in verse 27a, *Now you*, who are gathered in the unity of faith, *are Christ's body* (as Ephesians 1:22-23a says, *And he [God, the Father] put all things beneath his feet and gave him as head over all things to the Church, which is his body*). Then Paul applies the simile with respect to the differences among the members, by adding, in verse 27b, *and individually parts of it.*

This can be understood in three different ways. One sense is that you are all parts who depend on Christ, the first part; for he is called a member by reason of his humanity, and on this basis he is specifically called the head of the Church. But in his divinity he is not a member or a part of the Church, because he is the common good of the whole universe. A second sense of the phrase, *individually parts of it*, is that we are parts who are mutually dependent, since Paul in 4:15 of this same epistle says, *I became your father in*

Christ Jesus through the gospel, that is, he was the one who won the Corinthians for Christ. The third sense of the phrase, *individually parts of it*, is that it designates the differences and connections among the members, that is, they are distinguished and ordered among themselves mutually.

Then when Paul says in verse 28, *Some people God has designated in the Church to be* in specific offices, he goes on to treat of the differences among services and assigns a ranking of services, presenting first the major or principal administrative offices, and then the secondary ministries, beginning, in verse 28b, with *assistance*. Next, in verse 29, Paul shows the differences between these ministries; and finally, in verse 31, he indicates which of these different ministries should be preferred.

Now the major ministers in the Church are the apostles to whose office pertain three things: The first is the authority to govern the faithful—and this is proper to the apostolic office; the second is the faculty to teach; and the third is the power to work miracles in confirmation of this teaching. These three things are mentioned in Luke 9:1-2, *[Jesus] summoned the Twelve and gave them power and authority over all demons and to cure diseases, and he sent them to proclaim the kingdom of God and to heal the sick.*

In any orderly assignment of authority or power, that which is chief is reserved to the supreme office, while other powers are also shared with subordinates. Now the authority to work miracles is a means toward effective teaching as its end (as Mark 16:20 says, *They went forth and preached everywhere, while the Lord worked with them and confirmed the word through accompanying signs*); and teaching in turn is a means toward the governing of God's people as its end (as Jeremiah 3:15 says, *I will appoint over you shepherds after my own heart, who will shepherd you wisely and prudently*). Therefore, the highest position among ecclesiastical ministries is that of the apostles, and to them the governance of the Church pertains in a special way.

Hence, Paul says, *God has designated*, that is, assigned in a certain order, *some people in the Church* to definite offices (as John 15:16 says, *It was not you who chose me, but I who chose you and appointed you to go and bear fruit that will remain*): *first, apostles*, to whom he entrusted the direction of the Church (as Luke 22:29 says, *And I confer a kingdom on you, just as my Father has conferred one on me*, and in Revelation 21:14 it says of the heavenly Jerusalem, *The wall of the city had twelve courses of stones as its foundation, on which were inscribed the twelve names of the twelve apostles of the Lamb*).

Because of their supreme office, the Twelve also received a primacy in spiritual gifts in comparison to the rest of the faithful (as Romans 8:23 says, *We . . . who have the firstfruits of the Spirit*). And although the office of teaching pertains principally to the apostles, since it is to them that it was said (in Matthew 28:19-20) *Go, therefore, and make disciples of all nations . . . teaching them all that I have commanded you*, nevertheless others have been brought in to share in this office.

Some in the Church have personally received revelations from God, and they are called prophets, while some instruct the people in what has been revealed to others, and they are called teachers. And so Paul adds, *second, prophets* (since there are also prophets in the New Testament, and what is said in Matthew 11:13, *All the prophets and the law prophesied up to the time of John* [the Baptist] is to be understood as referring only to prophets of Christ's coming).

Paul continues, *third, teachers* (as Acts of the Apostles 13:1 says, *There were in the Church at Antioch prophets and teachers*). Similarly the grace of working miracles, which Christ had originally given to the apostles, was also communicated to others; so Paul adds, *then, mighty deeds*, which refers to those who work miracles over the very elements of the cosmos (so Galatians 3:5 speaks of the One *who works mighty deeds among you*). But with regard to miracles which take place in human bodies, Paul adds, *then gifts of healing* (as Luke 9:1 says, Christ gave them power *to cure diseases*).

When in verse 28b Paul lists gifts *of assistance*, however, he begins to mention the minor or secondary officials. Some are appointed to govern the Church (but as we have said, this properly pertains to the dignity of apostleship), while others are appointed to teach. Generally speaking, to the government of the Church pertain certain assistants, that is, those who aid the major officials in the universal government of the Church, for example, archdeacons (as Paul says in Philippians 4:3, *Yes, and I ask you also, my true comrade* to help them,** for they have struggled at my side in promoting the gospel, along with Clement and my other co-workers, whose names are in the book of life*).

For the local government of the Church Paul mentions administrators, for example, parish priests. To them the government of some local group of people is committed (for as Proverbs 11:14 says, *For lack of guidance a people fails; security lies in many counselors*). Of secondary offices those which pertain to teaching hold the second place, hence Paul adds, *varieties of tongues*, with reference to those who speak of the great things of God in various tongues, as is described in Acts of the Apostles 2:4, when they *began to speak in different tongues, as the Spirit enabled them to proclaim.* This grace is given so that the teaching of the gospel might not be impeded by the variety of ways in which people speak. Finally Paul asks in verse 30, *Do all interpret?* that is, remove the impediment which can come from the obscurity of sayings (later in this epistle at 14:13, he says, *Therefore one who speaks in tongues should pray to be able to interpret*).

Then, when Paul says in verse 29-30, *Are all apostles? Are all prophets? Are all teachers?* etc., he shows the differences among the services he has mentioned. The answer to each of these questions is understood to be no, yet the diversity of the offices is also implied (as Sirach 33:11 says, *Yet with his great knowledge the Lord made men unalike*, and Sirach 37:27 says, *For not every food is good for every one*).

In conclusion, when Paul says in verse 31, *Strive eagerly for the greatest spiritual gifts. But I shall show you a still more excellent way,* he sets in proper order the Corinthians' preferences for the spiritual gifts he has mentioned. While there are many gifts of the Holy Spirit, as has been said, *Strive eagerly for,* that is, desire, *the greatest spiritual gifts,* that is, the graces that are preferable; have a greater

---

* Syzygos, an unknown co-worker of Paul's.
** Euodia and Syntyche who were having a disagreement.

desire for those which are better, for example, prophecy rather than the gift of tongues (as he counsels later in this epistle, 14:1-4, and as 1 Thessalonians 5:21 says, *Test everything; retain what is good*).

And lest the Corinthians should desire only these ministerial gifts which he has been discussing, he adds, *But I shall show you a still more excellent way,* namely, love, since by love one is led more directly to God (as Psalm 119:32 says, *I will run the way of your commands, for you open my docile heart,* and Isaiah 30:21 says, *This is the way; walk in it*).

Graces
for Personal Holiness

Paul, after discussing the ministerial gifts in the service of the Church, which are only means to its holiness, now goes on to its goal, holiness itself. Thomas makes this chapter the basis of his entire teaching on the spiritual life, since union with God is accomplished not by special charisms, but by the theological virtues of faith, hope and love given to all Christians in baptism, and of these love is the supreme gift which constitutes Christian holiness and unifies the whole of Christian life. It should be noted that the term translated here by "love" is the Latin *charitas* (Greek *agape*), which is specifically Christian love of God and neighbor and not "love" in the sexual or other broader senses of the English word.

Commentary on Paul's First Epistle to the Corinthians

Chapter 13
Grace and Ministry

The Primacy of Love

Paul wants to show in this chapter that it is not the gifts of ministry that as such make us holy and Christ-like but the gifts of sanctifying grace and the theological virtues, above all love in which Christian perfection consists. *We give thanks to God always for all of you, remembering you in our prayers, unceasingly calling to mind your work of faith and labor of love and endurance in hope of our Lord Jesus Christ, before our God and Father* (1 Thes 1:2-3). *For we have heard of your faith in Christ Jesus and the love that you have for all the holy ones because of the hope reserved for you in heaven* (Col 1:4-5). This point is central to all that Thomas has to say about the Christian life. His long discursus on the angels is not out of place, although it takes off from a single word in Paul, because for Aquinas we humans are part of a very much greater family of spiritual beings who form God's kingdom of love. Our growing sympathy for the other world religions and especially for Native American religion is beginning to make us moderns more open to this idea of an all-encompassing spirit world.

¹If I speak in human and angelic tongues, but do not have love, I am a resounding gong or a clashing cymbal. ²And if I have the gift of prophecy, and comprehend all mysteries and all knowledge, if I have all faith so as to move mountains, but do not have love, I am nothing. ³If I give away [Latin: as food for the poor] everything I own, and if I hand my body over so that I may boast,* but do not have love, I gain nothing.

---

* Or "be burned," a reading considered more probable by many textual critics.

The Apostle Paul in chapter 12 pointed out the differences among the ministerial graces and ministries which differentiate the members of the Church. Now he deals with the virtue of love, which always accompanies personal, sanctifying grace. Since he promised at the end of chapter 12 to show the Corinthians *a more excellent way*, he now explains how love has preeminence over the ministerial gifts; first, because it is more necessary, since the ministerial gifts without love cannot save us; second, in verse 4, because love is more beneficial, since by it every evil is avoided and every good accomplished; and third, in verse 8, because ministry lasts only a lifetime, love forever.

In explaining these reasons, Paul seems to reduce the many ministerial gifts to three kinds. Thus, in verse 1 he shows that the gift of tongues, which pertains to speech, is of no avail without love. In verse 2 he shows that those gifts which pertain to knowledge are also of no avail without love. And in verse 3 he shows the same with regard to those gifts which pertain to action.

Among the Corinthians, the gift of tongues was considered highly desirable, as is clear from chapter 14 of this epistle, and so he begins with it and says, I promised to show you a more excellent way, and its excellence is evident first of all in comparison with the gift of tongues: Verse 1, *If I speak in human and angelic tongues*, that is, if by a gift of grace I am able to speak the languages of all peoples—and he adds, *angelic tongues*, to suggest an even greater gift, *but do not have love, I am a resounding gong or a clashing cymbal*.

This is a fitting comparison, for through love the soul lives by God himself, who becomes the very life of the soul (as Deuteronomy 30:19-20 says, *Choose life, then, that you and your descendants may live, by loving the Lord, your God, heeding his voice, and holding fast to him. For that will mean life for you*, and 1 John 3:14 says, *We know that we have passed from death to life because we love our brothers. Whoever does not love remains in death*). Paul is also right when he compares speech that lacks love to the sound of a non-living thing, such as a *resounding gong or a clashing cymbal* [Latin: *sounding brass or a ringing cymbal*]. These may indeed give forth a loud sound, yet they are dead, not living. So also is the speech of a person who lacks love: However eloquent it may be, it should nevertheless be considered dead, because it is of no use toward the meriting of eternal life.

But there is a difference between sounding brass and a ringing cymbal. Because it is flat, a piece of brass gives forth a simple sound when it is struck. On the other hand, a cymbal, because it is concave, when struck reverberates to produce a characteristically sustained sound. And so those who proclaim the truth in a simple way are like brass, while others are like cymbals. These latter, as it were, reverberate the truth and, when they proclaim it, add many reasons and similes and draw forth a great many conclusions. But without love all these words should be judged dead.

We should also consider what is meant by the *angelic tongues*. For the tongue is a bodily member and pertaining to its use there is also the gift of tongues, which is sometimes itself called a *tongue* (cf. 14:2, etc., of this epistle)—and neither of these things seem to be applicable to angels, who have no bodily members. It could be said that the *angels* here are to be understood to be human beings who have the office of angels, namely, that of announcing divine things to other human beings (as Malachi 2:7 says, *The lips of the priest are to keep knowledge, and instruction is to be sought from his mouth, because he is the messenger [angel] of the Lord of hosts*), and so in this sense, to *speak in human and angelic tongues* is said of all those who instruct others, not only the lesser teachers but also the greater.

This phrase can also be understood of the incorporeal angels themselves. Psalm 104:4 (Latin) says, *He makes his angels spirits*. Although angelic spirits do not have a bodily tongue, nevertheless by analogy they can be said to have a tongue in that they can reveal their own minds to others. But it should be known that within the knowledge of the angelic mind there is something about which higher angels do not speak to lower ones nor vice versa, namely, the divine Essence itself, which all the blessed see immediately, because God reveals himself to all of them (as Jeremiah 31:34 says, *No longer will they have need to teach their friends and kinsmen how to know the Lord. All from the least to the greatest, shall know me*).

Also in the knowledge of the angelic mind there are truths about which the higher angels do speak to the lower but not vice versa, such as the mysteries of divine providence. In seeing God the higher angels learn more about God's plan than do the lower angels, for they see him more clearly. And so the higher ones instruct or illuminate the lower ones about these things—and this can be called the *angelic tongues.*

Finally, within the knowledge of the angelic mind there are truths about which the higher angels cannot speak to the lower nor vice versa, such as the secrets of human hearts which depend upon free will, and these are evident to God alone and to the persons themselves (as 2:11 of this epistle says, *Among human beings, who knows what pertains to a person except the spirit of the person that is within?*). These things become known to an angel only when they are made freely known by that person whose secrets they are, whether that person is of lower rank or of higher than the one to whom he tells them.

Yet in the case of a lower angel, a manifestation of this sort takes place when he speaks to a higher one, not by illumination but by some kind of sign. In the mind of every angel there are truths which are naturally known by all other angels. When, therefore, what is naturally known is used as a sign of that which is unknown, a secret can be manifested. Manifestation of this sort are called the *angelic tongues* by analogy to that of human beings, for we make known to others the secrets of our hearts through sounds that can be perceived by the senses or through something else that is corporeal and outwardly sensible. Thus when those things which are naturally known among angels are employed for the manifestation of secrets, they are called signs or gestures, and the power to manifest their ideas in this way is called, metaphorically, a *tongue.*

Then, when Paul says in verse 2, *And if I have the gift of prophecy, and comprehend all mysteries and all knowledge, if I have all faith so as to move mountains, but do not have love, I am nothing,* he shows the preeminence of love with regard to gifts of knowledge. Recall that in chapter 12 he discussed four ministerial gifts that pertain to knowledge: wisdom, knowledge, faith and prophecy. First he speaks of prophecy here, saying, *And if I have the gift of prophecy.* By means of prophecy, secret things are revealed in a divine way (as 2 Peter 1:21 says, *For no prophecy ever came through human will, but rather human beings moved by the Holy Spirit spoke under the influence of God*).

Second, with regard to wisdom, Paul adds *comprehend all mysteries*, that is, the secrets of divinity, which pertain to wisdom (as we read in 2:7 of this same epistle, *We speak God's wisdom, mysterious, hidden, which God predetermined before the ages for our glory*).

Third, with regard to knowledge, he says *and all knowledge*, whether it has been acquired in a human fashion, such as the philosophers had, or infused in a divine fashion, like the apostles had (as Wisdom 7:17 says, *He gave me sound knowledge of existing things*).

Fourth, with regard to faith Paul adds, *if I have all faith, so as to move mountains. All faith* can be explained as faith in all the articles of the creed, but it is more likely that *all faith* means perfect faith, on account of what follows: *so as to move mountains;* because Jesus, in Matthew 17:20, says to the apostles, *If you have faith the size of a mustard seed, you will say to this mountain, "Move from here to there," and it will move.*

Granted that the mustard seed is very small in size, it is to be understood that the mustard seed is being compared, not to small faith, but to perfect faith, for Jesus, in Matthew 21:21, after he caused the fig tree to wither, says to the apostles, *If you have faith and do not waver, not only will you do what has been done to the fig tree, but even if you say to this mountain, "Be lifted up and thrown into sea," it will be done.* Thus an unhesitating faith is compared to a mustard seed: The finer it is ground, the more the strength of its odor and flavor is evident.

Of course some may object that, while many of the saints have had perfect faith, none of them is recorded to have moved mountains. But this difficulty can be explained by what was said earlier in 12:7, *To each individual the manifestation of the Spirit is given for some benefit.* For miracles take place by the grace of the Holy Spirit in the manner, place, and time which their usefulness for the

Church requires. Moreover, the saints have done much greater things than move mountains for the benefit of the faithful; for example, they have revived the dead, divided the sea, and done other works of this sort; and they could also move mountains, if the need were there.

Move mountains can also refer metaphorically to the expulsion of demons from human bodies, since because of their pride the devils are called mountains (as Jeremiah 13:16 says, *Give glory to the Lord your God . . . before your feet stumble upon darkening mountains*, and Jeremiah 51:25 says, *Beware! I am against you, destroying mountain, destroyer of the entire earth, says the Lord*). The working of miracles is attributed to a faith which does not hesitate, because faith rests upon the omnipotence of God through which miracles take place.

Paul says, if I have all the aforesaid gifts which pertain to the perfection of the intellect *but do not have love*, by which the will is perfected, *I am nothing*, as far as existence in saving grace is concerned, since in this regard, as Ephesians 2:10 says, *We are his handiwork, created in Christ Jesus for good works that God has prepared in advance, that we should live in them*, and also Ezekiel 27:36 says of the tyrannical city of Tyre, *You have become a horror, and you shall be no more*, because of its lack of love. Through love a person uses a trained intelligence well; without love the best intellect will be abused (as it is said in 8:1 of this epistle, *Knowledge inflates with pride; but love builds up*).

Note that here the apostle is speaking about wisdom and knowledge insofar as they pertain to the ministerial gifts, which can exist without love, but insofar as wisdom and other gifts of knowledge are counted among the seven gifts of the Holy Spirit, they are never had without love (as we read in Wisdom 1:4, *Because into a soul that plots evil wisdom enters not, nor dwells in a body under debt of sin*, and in Wisdom 10:10, *She [wisdom], when the just man [Jacob] fled from his brother's anger . . . showed him the kingdom of God and gave him the knowledge of holy things*). But with regard to prophecy and faith, it is clear that they can be possessed without love.

Also note in this regard that, even without love, a firm faith can work miracles. In Matthew 7:23, responding to those who say, *Have we not prophesied in your name and performed many great deeds?* Jesus says, *I never knew you.* For the Holy Spirit performs great deeds even through evil people, just as he also speaks the truth through them.

Then, when in verse 3a Paul says, *If I give away* [Latin: *as food for the poor*] *everything I own*, he shows the same to be true as regards those gifts which pertain to deeds. These are given that one might do good (as Galatians 6:9 says, *Let us not grow tired of doing good*) and patiently endure evil (as Psalm 92:15-16 says, *They shall bear fruit even in old age, always vigorous and sturdy, as they proclaim, "The Lord is just"*). Now above all other good works, deeds of piety are commended to us (as 1 Timothy 4:8 says, *Devotion is valuable in every respect*).

Paul points out four conditions with regard to these works of devotion. The first is that the deed of devotion not be concentrated on one person but be distributed among many (as Psalm 112:9 says, *Lavishly they give* [Latin: *distribute*] *to the poor*). This Paul indicates by saying, *If I give away*. The second is that the devout work be done for the relief of need and not in the service of excess (as Isaiah 58:7 says, *Sharing your bread with the hungry*). Paul indicates this by saying *as food*. The third is that the devout work be for those who are in need (as Luke 14:13 says, *When you hold a banquet, invite the poor, the crippled, the lame, the blind*). Paul indicates this by saying *for the poor*. The fourth is that it is a matter of perfection for a person to expend all of his goods on works of devotion (as Matthew 19:21 says, *If you wish to be perfect, go, sell what you have, and give it to the poor*). This Paul indicates by saying *everything I own*.

As regards verse 3b which reads, *And if I hand my body over so that I may boast [be burned], but do not have love, I gain nothing*, one should note that of all the evils that one might endure patiently, the greatest is martyrdom (as Matthew 5:10 says, *Blessed are they who are persecuted for the sake of righteousness*). Paul also commends this in four ways.

First, when the necessity is imminent, say, to defend the faith, it is more praiseworthy to expose oneself to suffering than only to suffer when caught, and so Paul says, *If I hand my body over* (as in Ephesians 5:2 it is also said of Christ that he *loved us and handed himself over for us as sacrificial offering to God*).

Second, the sacrifice of the human body is more serious than that of possessions (although in Hebrews 10:34 certain persons are commended for this also: *You joyfully accepted the confiscation of your property*), and so Paul says, *body* (as in Isaiah 50:6 says, *I gave my back to those who beat me*).

Third, it is more praiseworthy to expose one's own body to torment than to give up a son or any other relative to torment (yet in 2 Maccabees 7:20 a certain woman is commended for this too: *It seems admirable beyond measure and worthy of being remembered by all good people that she watched seven sons perish in the space of a single day and bore it in a good spirit*). Hence, Paul says *my body* (Judges 5:9, Latin, says, *You, who of your own will have exposed yourself to danger for the sake of the Lord*).

Fourth, martyrdom is rendered more praiseworthy by the harshness of the pain endured, so Paul adds *to be burned*, like Saint Lawrence (as Sirach 50:9 says, *Like the fire of incense at the sacrifice*). Paul concludes that if one should perform the works mentioned even in the most excellent manner *but do not have love*—either because along with the works mentioned there is present a will to sin mortally or because I do them for vainglory—*I gain nothing* to merit eternal life, because salvation is promised as a reward only to those who love God (as Job 36:33, Latin, says, *He tells his friend concerning the reward that will be his*).

Notice that in the case of speech, which is a sound of a living thing, if it is without love, Paul compares it to that which does not exist; but in the case of works, which are done for an end, if they are without love, he calls them unfruitful (as Wisdom 3:11 says, *Vain is their hope, fruitless are their labors, and worthless are their works*).

Love Made Perfect

Thomas is insistent that Christian love (in Greek *agape*, in Latin *charitas*) is not just any kind of love but the love of God for us, in which we share in living faith by grace and which extends to ourselves and our neighbors, because God loves us. We cannot directly know that our love for God is authentic, but through the Holy Spirit we are given signs of its presence in our lives. Paul, like a good spiritual director, describes these signs of authentic Christian love.

> [4]Love is patient, love is kind. It is not jealous, love is not pompous, it is not inflated, [5]it is not rude, it does not seek its own interests, it is not quick tempered; it does not brood over injury, [6]it does not rejoice over wrongdoing but rejoices with the truth. [7]It bears all things, believes all things, hopes all things, endures all things.

The Apostle Paul has shown that love is so necessary that without it no spiritual gift is sufficient for salvation. Now he shows it to be so useful and to have such effective power that by means of love all the works of virtue are performed. First, he begins in verse 4a by presenting two rather general observations; then, in verse 4b, he adds in a specific way the works of virtues which are brought to completion by love.

Since every virtue consists in conducting oneself well in enduring evil things or in doing good things, with regard to bearing evils, Paul says, *Love is patient,* that is, it makes one patient in bearing evils, for when persons love others they will easily bear any difficulty on account of their love. Likewise, one who really loves God will patiently bear with any adversity on account of that love (hence, Song of Songs 8:7 says, *Deep waters cannot quench love, nor floods sweep it away,* and James 1:4 says, *Let perseverance be perfect, so that you may be perfect and complete, lacking in nothing*). But with regard to doing good things, Paul adds, *Love is kind.* Kindness can be said to be a sort of "good fire."* Just as fire melts solids and

---

* By a play on the Latin *benigna,* "kind," and *bonus ignis,* "good fire."

causes them to diffuse, so love causes one not to hoard his goods just for oneself but to diffuse them among others (as Proverbs 5:16 says, *How may your water sources be dispersed abroad, streams of water in the streets?*). This indeed is what love does (as 1 John 3:17 says, *If someone who has worldly means sees a brother in need and refuses him compassion, how can the love of God remain in him?* and Ephesians 4:32 says, *Be kind to one another, compassionate,* and Wisdom 1:6 says, *For wisdom is a kindly spirit*).

Then, when Paul in verse 4c says, *love is not jealous,* he begins to describe in detail the works of the virtues that love brings about. Now two things pertain to virtue: to abstain from evil and to do good (as Psalm 34:15 says, *Turn from evil and do good,* and Isaiah 1:16d-17 says, *Cease doing evil; learn to do good*). Paul first shows how love makes a person avoid all evil deeds, then how it makes a person do all good deeds, when he says, *but rejoices with the truth.*

Human beings cannot effectively do evil to God but only to themselves or to their neighbors (as Job 35:6, 8 says, *If you sin, what injury do you do to God? . . . Your wickedness can affect only a man like yourself; and your justice only a fellow human being*). Paul, therefore, shows first of all how by means of love the se evils are avoided which are against one's neighbor, and then how those evils are avoided by which one loses one's own integrity, when he says, love *is not inflated.*

Evil which is against one's neighbor can be either in inward attitude or outward behavior. It is principally in inward attitude when through envy someone grieves over his neighbor's good fortune. This is directly contrary to love, since it pertains to love for one to love another as one's self, as it says in Leviticus 19:18, and so it pertains to love to rejoice over one's neighbor's good fortune just as over one's own. It follows from this that love excludes envy, and this is what is meant by love *is not jealous,* that is, does not begrudge, because love causes one to avoid envy (and so Psalm 37:1b says, *Do not envy those who do wrong,* and Proverbs 23:17 says, *Do not let your heart emulate sinners, but be zealous for the fear of the Lord always*).

With regard to outward behavior toward others Paul adds, *Love is not pompous*, that is, contemptuous of others. For no one acts disrespectfully toward one whom he loves as himself (as Isaiah 1:16 says, *Cease doing evil, learn to do good. Make justice your aim: redress the wronged, hear the orphan's pleas, defend the widow. Stop acting perversely*).

Then, when Paul says, love *is not inflated*, etc., he shows how love makes one avoid the evil desires by which one loses one's own inward integrity: first, with regard to passions, and then with regard to choice, when he says *love does not think evil*. And thus he shows first that love restrains disordered passion in three ways. First, love restrains pride, which is an inordinate desire for one's own excellence. We desire our own excellence in an inordinate way when we are not content with the rank in the universe provided for us by God (and so Sirach 10:14 says, *The beginning of man's pride is to separate himself from God*). This happens when a person does not want to be subject to the rule of the divine ordering of the universe. Now this is opposed to love, by which one loves God above all things (hence Colossians 2:18-19 condemns one who is *inflated without reason by his fleshly mind* and so not *holding closely to the head*, that is, Christ). For pride is justly compared to a kind of inflation, for that which is puffed up looks like a large solid object but is not. So indeed the proud seem to be great to themselves, even though they lack true greatness, which cannot exist outside the divine order (as Wisdom 4:19, Latin, says, *He will burst those who are puffed up and leave them speechless*).

The principal offspring of pride is ambition, by which one seeks to dominate others. Love excludes this also, for it chooses rather to serve its neighbors (as Galatians 5:13 says, *Serve one another through love*), and so Paul adds in verse 5, love *is not ambitious*,* that is, love makes one avoid ambition (as Sirach 7:4 says, *Seek not from the Lord authority, nor from the king a place of honor*).

Second, Paul shows how love drives back inordinate acquisitiveness, when he says, love *does not seek its own interests*. To

---

* Greek *aschemonei* simply means "dishonorable," but the Latin takes it to mean "ambitious" and NAB to mean "rude."

understand this more precisely: Love does not seek what is its own to the neglect of the good of others, for those who love others as themselves seek the good of others as well as of themselves. And so earlier, at 10:33 of this epistle, Paul said he was *not seeking my own benefit but that of the many, that they may be saved.* In contrast, in Philippians 2:21 he says of certain persons, *They all seek their own interests, not those of Jesus Christ.* Love *does not seek its own interests* can also be understood in another way, namely, that persons who love do not demand a return for those things of which they have been wrongly deprived, for example, by seeking judgment against their neighbor in a secular court and thus causing scandal, because they value their neighbor's salvation more than money (as Paul says in Philippians 4:17, *It is not that I am eager for [your] gift; rather, I am eager for the profit that accrues to your account*). This is to be understood in terms of what was said about lawsuits in chapter 6:1-11 of this epistle.

Third, Paul shows how love rules out inordinate anger, when he says, love *is not quick tempered,* that is, it is not easily provoked to anger. It pertains to love to forgive offenses rather than to avenge them beyond measure or inordinately (as Colossians 3:13 says, *. . . bearing with one another and forgiving one another, if one has a grievance against another; as the Lord has forgiven you, so must you do also,* and as James 1:20 says, *For the wrath of a man does not accomplish the righteousness of God*).

Then, when Paul says, love *does not brood over injury,* he shows how inordinate choice is excluded by love. As it says in Aristotle, Nicomachean Ethics III, choice is the desire for something that has been deliberately considered, for a person is said to sin by choice, rather than out of passion, when his desire for evil is aroused by reasoned deliberation. Love, therefore, first of all excludes evil deliberation. And so Paul says love *does not brood over injury,* that is, it does not allow itself to think about how it might accomplish evil (as Micah 2:1 says, *Woe to those who plan iniquity and work out evil on their couches,* and Isaiah 1:16 says, *Put away your misdeeds* [Latin: *evil thoughts*] *from before my eyes*). Or else, love *does not brood over injury,* because it does not allow a person to think evil of his neighbor through various suspicions and rash judgements (as Jesus says in Matthew 9:4, *Why do you harbor evil thoughts?*).

Second, love excludes any inordinate desire for evil things, hence Paul says in verse 6a, *love does not rejoice over wrongdoing*. One who sins out of passion commits sin with a certain remorse and sorrow, but one who sins by choice rejoices over the fact that he commits sin (as Proverbs 2:14 says, . . . *who delight in doing evil, rejoice in perversity*). But love prevents this, since it is love of the highest good, God, to whom every sin is repugnant. Or else Paul means, love *does not rejoice over wrongdoing* committed by a neighbor but rather mourns over it, since sin is contrary to the salvation of one's neighbors—which love desires (as 2 Corinthians 12:21 says, *I fear that when I come again my God may humiliate me before you, and I may have to mourn over many of those who sinned earlier and have not repented of the impurity, immorality, and licentiousness they practiced*).

Then, when Paul says in verse 6b, love *rejoices with the truth*, he shows how love makes one do good: first, with regard to neighbor; second, with regard to God, when he says, *believes all things*.

Now with regard to one's neighbor, one does good in two ways: first, by rejoicing over his good fortune; second, by enduring his evil deeds. With regard to good fortune, Paul says, *love rejoices with the truth*, that is, in hearing that neighbors truly prosper, whether in their lives or teaching or in virtue—because one loves one's neighbor as one's self (as 2 John 4 says, *I rejoiced greatly to find some of your children walking in the truth, just as we were commanded by the Father*).

The second way love does good is by enduring the evil deeds of a neighbor as one should. In this regard, Paul says in verse 7, love *bears all things*, that is, without being upset it endures all the defects of neighbors and any adversities whatsoever (as Romans 15:1 says, *We who are strong ought to put up with the failings of the weak and not to please ourselves*, and Galatians 6:2 says, *Bear one another's burdens and so you will fulfill the law of Christ*, namely, to love God and neighbor as oneself).

Then, when Paul says, in verse 7, love *believes all things*, he shows how love can make one do good in relation to God. Now this happens principally through the theological virtues, which have God as their object. Besides love, there are two other theological virtues, namely, faith and hope, as is said below in verse 13.

Hence, with regard to faith, he says, love *believes all things*, that is, all the things which have been divinely handed on to us (as Genesis 15:6 says, *Abraham put his faith in the Lord, who credited it to him as an act of righteousness*). But to believe all the things which are said by a human being is lightmindedness (as Sirach 19:4, Vulgate, says, *He who lightly trusts in them [bad companions] has no sense*).

Then with regard to hope, he says, love *hopes all things*, that is, for all the good things which have been promised by God (as Sirach 2:9 says, *You who fear God hope for good things, for lasting joy and mercy*). And lest hope be shattered by delay, he adds, love *endures all things*, that is, patiently awaits the things promised by God however long they may be delayed (as Habakkuk 2:3 says of God's promise, *If it delays, wait for it, it will surely come; it will not be late*, and Psalm 27:14 says, *Wait for the Lord, take courage; be stouthearted, wait for the Lord*).

Love Lasts Forever

Thomas teaches that we cannot love persons without knowing something of them, and the more intimately we know them the deeper our love can grow; though it is also true that love can grow faster than knowledge. For Aquinas' love in the will drives the intellect to seek to know the beloved ever more intimately and rests only in perfect knowledge of the beloved. Thus love of God begins and ends in knowing God, since we can be finally and perfectly united to God only in the intimacy of vision. Hence, Aquinas differs from the Franciscan school of spirituality for which the beatific union with God terminates not in vision but in love, for which vision is merely the means. Yet, both the Franciscan and Dominican schools follow Paul's teaching that in this life Christian perfection consists in love, since love alone transcends death. A discursus by Aquinas defends the survival after death of the intellectual knowledge acquired in this life in the soul before the resurrection, although we will not regain our sensible memories until the resurrection, unless they are supplied to the separated soul by

God. This is important to the insistence in Dominican spirituality on the value of study. The vision of God is not a blinding light that eliminates all earthly knowledge. Rather, our earthly experience is retained and transformed in God's perfect light.

> [8]Love never fails. If there are prophecies, they will be brought to nothing; if tongues, they will cease; if knowledge, it will be brought to nothing. [9]For we know partially, and we prophesy partially, [10]but when the perfect comes, the partial will pass away. [11]When I was a child, I used to talk as a child, think as a child, reason as a child; when I became a man, I put aside childish things.

The Apostle Paul has shown that love surpasses the other gifts of the Holy Spirit in terms both of necessity and of fruitfulness. Now he shows how love excels the other gifts with regard to permanence. He does this in three steps: First, in verse 8, he points out that there is a difference between love and the other gifts, because love is permanent and the others are not. Then, in verses 9-12, he proves this; and in verse 13 he draws his conclusion.

And so he begins by saying in verse 8a, *Love never fails*. Some people have understood this wrongly and have fallen into error, for they say that, once possessed, love can never be lost. This seems to be in harmony with what 1 John 3:9 says, *No one who is begotten by God commits sin, because God's seed remains in him; he cannot sin because he is begotten by God.*

But first of all such an understanding of this saying is false, because someone who has love can fall away from love through sin (as Revelation 2:4b-5 says, *You have lost the love you had at first. Realize how far you have fallen. Repent, and do the works you did at first*). This is because love is received into a human soul according to the soul's own mode; the soul can either make use of the virtue of love or not. When one does indeed make use of love, one cannot sin. This is because to use love is to love God above all things; then there is no longer anything for the sake of which the person will offend God. This is the way in which the words quoted from John are to be understood.

Furthermore, the opinion mentioned is not in keeping with the apostle's intention, because here he is speaking not about the destruction of spiritual gifts through mortal sin but rather about the ending of the spiritual gifts which pertain to this life when glory comes upon us. What Paul means is that *Love never fails* because it will continue in heaven, as it is now on our way to heaven—only it will increase (as Isaiah 31:9 says, *Thus said the Lord, whose fire is in Zion*, that is, in the Church on earth, *and whose furnace is in Jerusalem*, the city of peace, that is, in the peace of the heavenly fatherland).

Then Paul sets forth the cessation of the other spiritual gifts and especially of those which seem to be the principal ones. First of all, with regard to prophecy he says in verse 8b, *If there are prophecies, they will be brought to nothing*, that is, will cease. Indeed, in future glory there will be no place for prophecy for two reasons. One reason is that prophecy looks to the future, but in heaven we will not be waiting for the future; rather, all those things which had been prophesied earlier will be finally completed (as Psalm 48:9 says, *What we had heard*, that is, through the prophets, *we now see as actually present in the city of the Lord of hosts*). Another reason that prophecy will cease is that it involves knowledge that is symbolic and obscure (as Numbers 12:6 says, *Should there be a prophet among you, in visions I will reveal myself to him, in dreams will I speak to him*, and Hosea 12:11 says, *I granted many visions and spoke to the prophets through whom I set forth examples*), and this obscurity will be removed by the vision of God.

Second, with regard to the gift of tongues Paul says, *if tongues, they will cease*. Of course, he does not mean the bodily members themselves which we call tongues; later in this epistle, 15:52 he writes, *The dead will be raised incorruptible*, that is, without loss of bodily members. Nor does he mean the use of the bodily tongue, for in our future homeland there will still be vocal praise, according to the *Gloss* on Psalm 149:6, *With the praise of God in their mouths*. Rather, Paul is referring to the gift of tongues. By means of this gift some persons in the primitive Church were able to speak in a variety of languages (as told in Acts of the Apostles 2:4-13). But in future glory every person will be able to understand any language whatsoever, and so it will not be necessary to speak in a variety of languages. Genesis 11:1 says that at the very beginning of the human race *the whole world spoke the same language, using the same words.* All the more will this be true in the final state of the human race, when unity will be brought to its consummation. Third, with regard to knowledge, Paul adds, *if knowledge, it will be brought to nothing.*

From these words certain people have wanted to assume that knowledge acquired in this life is totally destroyed when the body is destroyed. But to investigate the truth of this, note that the power to know is twofold: There is a sense power and an intellectual power, and there is a difference between the two: Sense powers are the actions of a bodily organ, and so must cease when the body decays; but the intellectual power is not the action of any bodily organ (as Aristotle proves in *De Anima III*), and so the intellect must remain even after the body decays. Therefore, if any acquired knowledge is preserved in the intellectual part of the soul, it must continue on after death.

Others have argued that concepts exist in the intelligence only when it is actually thinking, while sense images are preserved in the imagination and sense memory; hence, whenever the intellect wants to understand something anew, including even that which it has understood before, it needs again by its intellectual power to abstract these concepts from the preserved sense images. Therefore, intellectual knowledge acquired in this life does not remain after death.

This argument, however, is first of all contrary to reason. It is obvious that concepts are received in the intellect at least while it is actually understanding some object. But whatever is received in something is received according to the mode of the receiver. And so, if the substance of the intellect is unchangeable and fixed, then intellectual concepts should remain in it in a permanent way.

Secondly, this position does not agree with the teaching of Aristotle, a recognized authority on psychology. In *De Anima III*, he says that when the intellect is in the process of knowing something, it must have at the same time the power to know it. Clearly, then, even when the intelligence possesses the concepts by which it is actually knowing, it retains the power to know them. Thus, even when the intellect is not actually thinking of something, it already knows, it retains the concepts by which it is able to know that thing when it turns its attention to it. Hence also, in the same passage the philosopher says that the intellectual part of the soul is the place of concepts, because that is where concepts are preserved. Nevertheless in this mortal life the intellect needs sense images in order to actually know anything, not only to abstract concepts from images but also to apply to sense images the concepts it already has. A sign of this is that when the organ of imagination or memory is injured, the person is impeded not only from acquiring new knowledge but also from using knowledge already gained.

Therefore, after the death of the body knowledge does remain in the soul in terms of intellectual concepts but no longer in dependence on sense images. Instead, the soul once separated from the body will not need sense images, since it is able to exist and act without being in union with the body. Hence, when the Apostle Paul says here that knowledge will be destroyed, he refers only to such knowledge as is dependent on reference to sense images (as Isaiah 29:14 also says, *The wisdom of its wise men shall perish and the understanding of its prudent men be hid*).

Next, when in verse 9 Paul says, *For we know partially*, he proves what he has said about the permanence of love compared with the other gifts. First he presents the proof, then he makes what is contained in the proof more clear in verse 11.

To prove his point Paul begins by reasoning as follows: When that which is perfect appears, the imperfect ceases; but the gifts other than love do involve imperfection; therefore, they cease when the perfection of glory appears. The minor proposition he presents first with regard to the imperfection of knowledge, *For we know partially*, that is, imperfectly, for *part* implies incompletion, which is especially true with respect to our knowledge of God (as Job 36:26 says, *Lo, God is great, beyond our knowledge; the number of his years* is past searching out, and again 26:14, *Lo, these are but the outlines of his ways, and how faint is the word we hear!*).

Paul also points out the imperfection of prophecy, *And we prophesy partially*, that is, imperfectly. As was said earlier, prophecy is knowledge involving imperfection, since prophecies require interpretation. Note here that Paul is silent about the gift of tongues, but it is a less perfect gift than the two, knowledge and prophecy, which he has treated, as will be evident later on in chapter 14.

Next, Paul sets up the major premise of his proof, saying, *But when the perfect comes*, that is, the perfection of glory, *the partial will pass away*, that is, all imperfection will be taken away (as 1 Peter 5:10 says, *The God of all grace who called you to his eternal glory through Christ Jesus will himself restore, confirm, strengthen and establish you after you have suffered a little*). But in accord with this reasoning it might appear that love also will be put aside with the arrival of future glory, for love itself in this state of earthly exile is imperfect when it is compared with love in the conditions of our heavenly homeland.

Therefore, it should be said that imperfection is related in two different ways to that which is called imperfect. Sometimes imperfection pertains to the very nature of that which is imperfect, but sometimes this is not so, and imperfection is only accidental to what is imperfect. For example, imperfection is of the very nature of a child but not of the nature of a human being, and so, when the age of maturity arrives, childhood ceases, but human nature becomes perfect. Now imperfection is of the very nature of the knowledge which we have here about God, for he is known from things that we can sense. It is also of the very nature of prophecy, for it is symbolic knowledge, aimed toward the future.

But it is not of the very nature of love to be imperfect; for love requires that we love a good that is known, imperfectly or, better still, perfectly. And so when the perfection of glory arrives, prophecy and knowledge cease; love on the other hand does not cease but is instead brought to perfection—the more perfectly God is known, the more perfectly he is loved.

In verse 11 Paul says, *When I was a child, I used to talk as a child, think as a child, reason as a child; when I became a man, I put aside childish things,* and then he clarifies both premises of his proof. First, he clarifies the major (when the perfect arrives, the imperfect ceases); second, in verse 12, he clarifies the minor (knowledge and prophecy are imperfect).

He clarifies his major premise in terms of an analogy of perfect and imperfect as found in bodily age. First, he presents the imperfect in terms of bodily age, *When I was a child, I used to talk as a child,* that is, in a way that is typical of a child, in baby-talk. On account of the natural deficiency in speech which is found in children, in Wisdom 10:21 wisdom is commended because it has *opened the mouths of the dumb, and given ready speech to infants.* One who speaks silly things is said to speak like a child (as Psalm 12:3, Latin, says, *Everyone has spoken vain things to his neighbor*). With regard to judgment, Paul adds, *[I used to] think as a child,* that is, I approved and disapproved of some things in a foolish manner, the way children do. They sometimes have contempt for things which are precious and prize things which are of little worth (as Proverbs 1:22 says, *How long, simple ones, will you love inanity?*). And so, those who have contempt for spiritual things and cling to earthly things think like children (as Philippians 3:19 says of them, *Their glory is in their "shame." Their minds are occupied with earthly things*). With regard to discursive reasoning, Paul says, *[I] reason as a child,* that is, think about foolish things (as Psalm 94:11 says, *The Lord does know human plans, they are only puffs of air*).

Paul here seems to be putting these three items in inverted order, for speaking presupposes the judgment of wisdom, and judgment the thoughts of reason. But this order is quite in keeping with the imperfection of children, for they exercise speech without judgment and judgment without deliberation. It can also be that *I used to talk as a child* refers to the gift of tongues, *think as a child* to the gift of prophecy, and *reason as a child* to the gift of knowledge.

Next, Paul writes about what pertains to the perfection of age. He says, *When I became a man,* that is, when I came to the mature age of a grown man (as Isaiah 65:20 says of the inhabitants of the restored Jerusalem, *He dies a mere youth who reaches but a hundred years, and he who fails of a hundred shall be thought accursed),* I put aside childish things. Note that the apostle is here comparing our present state because of its imperfection to childhood but the state of future glory because of its perfection to the age of a mature man.

Love and Vision

Thomas understands Christian faith not simply as a "leap in the dark" but as supremely reasonable, since it relies not on frail human experience but on truth itself, God as he reveals himself to us through his Incarnate Word. Faith is a gift of grace by which, hoping for salvation, the will freely moves the intellect to consent to God's revelation, warranted to do so by signs accessible to our experience and reason, namely, by the fulfillment of prophecies, by miracles, by the power of the gospel to meet our deepest human needs, and most accessibly by the moral miracle of the one, holy, catholic, and apostolic Church. Although faith is obscure, it truly touches God and continues to grow until it becomes mystical contemplation, the dawn of the eternal light of glory. Important in this section, too, is Thomas' defense of the immediate vision of God in glory, a point which is obscure in Eastern mysticism, where the incomprehensibility of God led to Gregory Palamas' theory that even in heaven God will be known only by his "uncreated energies," not in the divine essence.

> [12]At present we see indistinctly, as in a mirror, but then face to face. At present I know partially; then I shall know fully, as I am fully known. [13]So faith, hope, love remain, these three; but the greatest of these is love.

Paul, in verse 12-13, speaks of that vision which is the knowledge of God. The fact that all the preceding gifts are to be put aside can be understood in that they are ordered to the knowledge of God as means to an end. In this regard Paul makes two observations: In verse 12a he shows what he has in mind in a general way and then, in verse 12b, applies this to himself.

Paul has already said that we know only in part. The reason for this is given in verse 12a, *At present we see indistinctly, as in a mirror, but then face to face.* But what does it mean to see *indistinctly, as in a mirror?* And what does it mean to see *face to face?* Note that there are three ways in which something sensible can be seen: first, by its own presence in the seer, the way light itself is present in the eye; second, by the presence of an image in the eye derived directly from the thing seen. This is the way the whiteness of a wall is seen; it is not whiteness itself which actually exists in the eye but an image of it, even if this image is not itself the object seen but only the medium through which it is seen. Third, by the presence of an image not directly derived from the thing itself but from an image of the thing in something else, the way somebody is seen reflected in a mirror. In the last case it is not the image of a person which is present in the eye but the image of that person reflected from a mirror.

These three modes of sensible sight can be analogically applied to the spiritual vision of God. By natural knowledge only God sees himself. In God his essence and his intellect are identical, and therefore his essence is immediately present to his intellect (this is analogous to the first of the three ways just mentioned, that is, as light is in the eye). Probably it is in the second way that the angels see God by natural knowledge, insofar as a likeness of the divine essence is present in them connaturally. But it is in the third way that we see God in this life. We know the invisible things of God by means of created beings, as Romans 1:20 says, *Ever since the creation of the world, God's invisible attributes of eternal power and divinity have been able to be understood and perceived in what he has made,* and so the whole of creation is a kind of mirror for us. From the order and goodness and greatness which God causes in things we come to a knowledge of the divine wisdom, goodness, and preeminence—and this knowledge can be said to be seen *as in a mirror.*

Note also that a likeness of this sort, a likeness which is reflected from another thing, is of two kinds. Sometimes it is plain and clear, like that in a clean mirror, and sometimes it is dim and hidden, like that in some dirty mirror, and then the vision is called "enigmatic," as when I [propose the riddle or enigma], "My mother bore me, but she is born of me," the meaning is hidden through a similitude to which the correct answer is, "ice," because ice is born from water when it is frozen, and from ice water is born when it is melted. Thus it is evident how vision through a likeness of a likeness can be in a mirror like a meaning hidden in a enigma [or riddle], while a clear and plain likeness produces another sort of vision although one which is still only a likeness [not the object itself].*

Or to interpret this in another way, *At present we see . . . as in a mirror* means "only through our reason," that is we "see" only by means of a power of our soul. With regard to the phrase *face to face,* we know that God, insofar as he is God, does not have a face, and so *face to face* is said metaphorically. When we see something in a mirror, we see not the thing itself but its likeness; but when we see something face to face, we see the thing itself, just as it is. And so when Paul says that in heaven we will see *face to face,* he means that we will see nothing other than the very essence of God (as 1 John 3:2 says, *Beloved, we are God's children now; what we shall be has not yet been revealed. We do know that when it is revealed we shall be like him, for we shall see him as he is*).

Now is this not contradicted in Genesis 32:31, where Jacob, after his wrestling match with the mysterious stranger *named the place Peniel, "Because I have seen God face to face . . . yet my life has been spared"?* Yet, certainly Jacob did not see the essence of God at that time, and so to see *face to face* does not necessarily mean to see the essence of God.

To this difficulty it should be replied that Jacob's vision was in his imagination. But such an imaginary vision, in which something is seen as present, is thought to be a revelation of a higher type than a much lower kind of revelation in which only words are heard. So to imply the excellence of the imaginary vision that was shown

---

* Inasmuch, therefore, as we know the invisible things of God analogically through created beings, we see them in a clean mirror; but insofar as they remain mysteries we see them "in an enigma." Thus Paul maintains in Romans 1:20 that God's existence is *evident* to all through his creation, but Thomas adds that this knowledge is still only analogical (a *visio allegorica* or "figurative vision").

him, Jacob says, *I have seen God face to face*, that is, "I have seen the Lord appearing in my imagination, in his image, although not in his essence."

Also others claim that in heaven we will see the divine essence itself only by means of a created likeness. But this is altogether false and indeed impossible. Something can never be known in its essence by means of a likeness which does not correspond to that thing specifically. A stone cannot be known as it truly is except by means of a specific likeness of the stone in the soul. No likeness can lead to the knowledge of the essence of anything if it differs from that thing in species—and much less if it differs in genus. Through the likeness of a horse or of whiteness, one cannot know the essence of a human being—much less the essence of an angel. Still less can one see the divine essence through any created likeness, whatever it may be. Any created likeness in the soul would be further from the divine essence than the likeness of a horse or of whiteness is from the essence of an angel. And so to assert that God is seen only by means of a likeness or some kind of refulgence of his splendor is to assert that the divine essence is not really seen.

Furthermore, since the soul is a kind of likeness of God, the bright and clear vision which is promised to the saints in glory (and in which our happiness consists) would be as mirror-like and obscure as the vision which we have on our earthly pilgrimage. This is why Augustine is quoted on this verse in the *Gloss* as saying that the vision of God by means of a likeness pertains to a vision in a mirror or an enigma. If in heaven we only saw God in an image it would also follow that the final happiness of human beings would consist in something other than God himself—which is contrary to the faith. Furthermore, the natural human desire to reach the first cause of all things and to know it as it is in itself would be in vain.

Next is verse 12b, *At present I know partially; then I shall know fully, as I am fully known.* What he has already proved in a general way, Paul now proves in a specific way in terms of his own knowledge of himself. He says, *At present*, in this earthly life, *I know partially*, that is, in an obscure and imperfect way; *but then*, in our homeland, *I shall know fully, as I am fully known,* that is, I will know God in his essence, just as God knows my essence ("as" here means only that the two knowledges are similar, not that they are equally perfect; God knows me better than I know myself or can know God even in heaven).

Finally, in verse 13, Paul draws his principal conclusion when he says, *So faith, hope, love remain, these three; but the greatest of these is love.* He does not mention all the other gifts but only these three. The reason for this is that these three unite us to God; the others do not unite us to God except by mediation of these three. Furthermore, the other gifts are certain disposing factors to bring these three to birth in our hearts. These three alone, faith, hope, and love, are also called "theological" virtues, because they have God as their immediate object.

It can be objected that God's gifts are for the perfection either of the will or of the intellect. Love perfects the will and faith the intellect, so hope does not seem to be necessary but rather superfluous. This can be answered if we recall that our relation to God is twofold. One relation is through the goods of nature, of which he gives us a share during this life; the other relation is through being transformed by grace, since through grace we share in the blessedness of heaven even during this life, insofar as it is possible here. We also hope to come to the perfect attainment of that eternal beatitude and to become citizens of the heavenly Jerusalem. Following upon that first relation with God there is a natural friendship, according to which everything insofar as it exists seeks God as the First Cause and the highest good and desires him as its end. But following upon the second relation there is the love of charity (agape), and it is only by this Christian love that the intelligent created being loves God as a friend.

Now nothing can be loved unless it is known, and so for Christian love the knowledge of God is needed first. Because this is something above nature, there is a need, first of all, for faith, which has to do with things not seen. Then, lest we fail or lose our way, there is a need for hope. By means of hope we tend toward that goal, namely God, as something which truly belongs to us as human persons. Sirach 2:8-10, Latin, speaks about these three virtues: as regards faith, *You who fear the Lord, believe in him;* as regards hope, *You who fear God, hope in him;* as regards love, *You who fear God, love him.** It is these three, therefore, that now remain. But, for the reason given, love is greater than all of them.

* This Latin verse is not in the NAB or JB, but in verses 15-16 we have, *Those who fear the Lord disobey not his words, those who love him keep his ways. Those who fear the Lord seek to please him, those who love him are filled with his law.*

The Cardinal Virtues

Although for Thomas spirituality especially concerns the theological virtues of faith, hope and love, which unite us directly to
God, these virtues cannot be active in us unless assisted by the
moral virtues, which deal with the main problems of earthly human life. While we acquire these virtues by human effort, they can
serve the theological virtues only when healed and transformed by
grace, that is, by corresponding infused virtues given to us in
baptism and conversion. The following selection from Aquinas'
Disputed Questions is one of his most succinct summaries of his
understanding of these virtues and how they mediate between our
human psychology and the basic difficulties of human life common to all times and places. Any spirituality which seeks mystical
experience without basing prayer on a disciplined life of virtues,
by which we are made truly human and able to relate well to our
human community in daily life, is a snare and a delusion.

A Disputed Question
on the Cardinal Virtues

(1, a. 1 c.)

Ambrose, commenting on Luke 6:20, *Blessed are the poor,* says, "We know that there are four cardinal virtues: temperance, justice, prudence and fortitude."

It should be said that these virtues are called "cardinal" from the Latin for the "hinge" on which a door swings, according to Proverbs 26:14, *The door turns on its hinges, as the sluggard on his bed.* Whence those virtues are called cardinal on which hangs, as it were, the door through which one enters into a truly human life, that is, a life lived according to human nature.

In human nature is found first, senses like those of other animals; second, practical reason, which is proper to humanity according to its place in the universe; and third, contemplative intelligence, in which, though we do not possess it as perfectly as the angels, our human souls in their own way participate.

Thus, the contemplative life is properly not human but superhuman; while the life of pleasure, which occupies itself with sensual goods, is not human either, but bestial. The life which is specifically human, therefore, is the active life, which consists in the exercise of the moral virtues. Therefore, those virtues are rightly called "cardinal" on which the moral life somehow hangs and turns, because they are the principles of a life of human action. For this reason they are also called the "principal" virtues.

Note, however, that there are things that pertain to the essence of a virtuous life. First, that the basic character of these acts should be intrinsically qualified. Hence, an act is said to be good, as it deals with the right problems or takes place in the right circumstances. Second, that the act may be rightly related to the agent, so that it is firmly planted in the agent. Third, that the act be rightly related to something outside the subject as its goal.

The first three of these qualify the acts which are directed by reason. The fourth, however, qualifies the reason which is itself directive, namely, its cognition. Aristotle touches on these four aspects of virtue when he says in the *Nicomachean Ethics II*, chapter 3, that it is a necessary but not sufficient condition of virtue that its act be rightly or temperately moderated. Yet, three other qualifications are required on the part of a moral agent. First, agents must know what they are doing, which pertains to the directive cognition. Second, the agents must choose deliberately to act for an appropriate end, and this pertains to the rightness of the act in relation to something extrinsic. Third, the agents must act firmly and unwaveringly.

Therefore, these four modes, namely directive [or practical] cognition, moderation, rightness and firmness are found in all the virtues, but each one predominates in respect to specifically different objects and acts. On the part of practical cognition three things are required: first, to take counsel; second, to judge concerning what has been counseled (just as theoretical cognition after investigation or inquiry then judges); third, on the basis of this deliberation, to judge what is to be done (since, as Aristotle says in *De Anima III*, practical reason, unlike theoretical intelligence, commands one to avoid or pursue something).

As to the first, we are perfected by the virtue of deliberating well about what is to be done (*eubulia*); as to the second by the virtue of judging by common rules of good behavior (*synesis*) or in unusual cases by higher ethical principles (*gnome*), as Aristotle says in the *Nicomachean Ethics VI*, chapter 10. But through *prudence*, as it is also said there, we are able not only to judge rightly but to command ourselves to actually execute our good judgments. Whence it is manifest that to *prudence* pertains what is principal in directive knowing, and therefore for this reason prudence is rated as a cardinal virtue.

Likewise, the rightness of an act in relation to an extrinsic end has a certain character of being good and praiseworthy even in matters that pertain to oneself, but is more praised in matters which are in relation to others, namely, when one rectifies one's own actions not only in those matters which pertain to oneself but also in those in which one has common interests with others. For Aristotle says in the *Nicomachean Ethics IV*, chapter 1, that many are able to act virtuously in their own affairs but are not able to do so in relation to others. For this reason, therefore, *justice* is considered a principal virtue by which one is duly adjusted and related as an equal to others with whom one shares community, since something is commonly called "adjusted" which is neatly fitted to something else.

Moderation (*temperance*), or restrain is chiefly praised and considered good in matters where passion is especially compulsive, which reason should restrain so that the middle course of virtue is attained. Now the strongest passions are those which drive us to pursue the greatest pleasures; and therefore *temperance* is a cardinal virtue which restrains the desire for pleasures of touch, that is, in food, drink, and sex.

Firmness especially is praised and considered good in situations where fear moves us to flight; and this especially in the greatest perils, which are mortal; and therefore *fortitude* (*courage*) is considered a cardinal virtue by which one acts fearlessly in the face of death.

Of these four virtues, prudence is in the reason, justice is in the will, fortitude is in the aggressive drives, and temperance in the drives for pleasure, which psychological powers alone are able to be principles of human acts, that is to be voluntary.

Thus it is clear why these are cardinal virtues: first, because of their ways of being virtues (that is, their formal specifying characteristics); second, because of the important problems with which they deal; and third, because of the psychological powers which they perfect.

The Holy Spirit's
Seven Gifts

A special note of the Dominican tradition to which Thomas belonged has always been a great interest in the seven gifts of the Holy Spirit. His own thought on this subject developed considerably, moving from the idea that these gifts are needed only for crises in our lives to his final view that they are required at every moment in authentic Christian living. They are necessary to free us from the stroke-by-stroke-rowing-a-boat mode of acting, characteristic of human nature, to that spontaneous, "graceful," Christlike mode of acting in which the Holy Spirit moves us like a boat gliding along with sails spread to the wind, which alone will bring us safely to harbor in God. These seven gifts operate in every Christian in grace, but become evident only in the saints.

Jacques Maritain,* basing himself on this thought of Aquinas, showed that a natural mysticism exists which is achievable by the practices of disciplines of meditation, such as yoga, whose goal is an experiential awareness of the spirituality of our own soul. (This is not, of course, to deny that grace may also be at work in these otherwise purely natural spiritual practices.) After death, this natural introverted awareness will become immediate and positive, but in this life it can only be a negative experience of the "void," that is, of an empty but spiritual self-awareness, what the Buddhists

---

* "Natural Mysticism and the Void," in *Redeeming the Time* (London: The Centenary Press, 1943), pp. 225-55.

85

called "nirvana" or the "blowing-out" of all images and concepts and the desires they arouse. It seems similar to the state of prayer advocated by Christian quietists, but which is not in fact really Christian.

Christian contemplative prayer, however, although it too has a natural psychological element, is principally a work of grace and consists essentially in acts of the supernatural gifts of faith, hope and love, as these take on an increasingly inspired mode through submission to the action of the Holy Spirit, made possible by his seven gifts, but especially by the intellectual gifts of understanding (insight), knowledge (science), and wisdom.

When the theological virtues act in the divine mode given by the gifts of the Holy Spirit, the Christian becomes co-natural to Christ, who is truly human yet truly God, as one violin string vibrates sympathetically in tune with another. It is above all the likeness to God produced by love and the gift of wisdom which enables the lover of God to know God through a profound empathy of faith. Authentic Christian mysticism consists in this infused contemplation, the dawn in this life of the full daylight of the beatific vision of the Trinity.

Commentary on the Book of the Prophet Isaiah

Chapter 11

The Hebrew text of Isaiah 11:2 mentions only six gifts. Some critics think that "and his delight shall be the fear of the Lord" is a gloss, but the Greek Bible (LXX) and the Latin Vulgate have "piety" instead of the first "fear of the Lord," thus making seven gifts. In Revelation 5:6, John beholds *A Lamb that seemed to have been slain. He had seven horns and eyes; these are the seven spirits of God sent out into the whole world*, that is, Christ endowed with the seven gifts of the Holy Spirit which emanate from him. In any case in biblical symbolism "seven" means "plenitude." Aquinas' identification of seven gifts depends on his explanation of the three theological and four cardinal virtues to which they correspond. "Piety" (*eusebeia* in Greek), "reverence," or "devotion" is certainly an important Christian virtue; the noun is used fourteen times in the New Testament, for example, in 1 Timothy 4:8-9, *For while physical training [asceticism] is of limited value, devotion [eusebeia] is valuable in every respect since it holds a promise of life, both for the present and the future. This saying is trustworthy and deserves full acceptance.*

> [2] The spirit of the Lord shall rest upon him;
> a spirit of wisdom and of understanding,
> A spirit of counsel and of strength,
> a spirit of knowledge and of fear of the Lord,
> and the spirit of the Lord will fill him,
> and his delight shall be the fear of the Lord.

The spirit of the Lord shall rest upon him. Here the prophet describes the holiness of the Messiah . . . and shows the perfection in three respects of the graces he will possess: first, as to their completeness with the phrase *shall rest*, since his grace did not increase (as it says in Jeremiah 31:22, *The woman will encompass the* man*); nor was his grace ever interrupted by sin (as Isaiah 53:9, quoted by 1 Peter 2:22, says, *He committed no sin, and no deceit was found in his mouth*); nor was his grace ever troubled by the war of the spirit and the flesh, since he was without original sin. (Thus Job 3:9 says [of himself as a member of the fallen human race], *Perish the day on which I was born. . . . May the stars of its twilight be darkened; may it look for daylight, and have none, nor gaze on the eyes of the dawn.* But [God says to John the Baptist concerning Jesus] in John 1:33, *On whomever you shall see the Spirit come down and remain, he is the one who will baptize with the Holy Spirit*).

Second, he shows the perfection of Christ's graces as to their number in comparison with all possible graces mentioned in the rest of the verse. For although all the graces of personal sanctification are infused simultaneously, nevertheless one individual cannot have the perfect use of all (hence in Sirach 44:20 it is said only of Abraham that he *kept his glory without stain*). Nor can one individual have all the ministerial graces (as it says in 1 Corinthians 12:8, *To one is given through the Spirit the expression of wisdom; to another the expression of knowledge according to the same Spirit*, etc.). But Christ had all these graces without exception (as John 3:34 says, *For God does not ration his gift of the Spirit*).

Third, he shows the perfection of Christ's graces as to their plenitude, since he not only had all graces but had them in fullness, which is noted in the phrase *will fill him* (as John 1:14 says, *And we saw his glory, the glory of the Father's only Son, full of grace and truth*, and Colossians 2:9 confirms, *For in him dwells the whole fullness of the deity bodily*).

To clarify what has been said in this verse it is necessary to see five things about these gifts. First, how they differ from the beatitudes and fruits; second, their number; third, their order; fourth, how they exist in Christ; fifth, how they are attributed to the Holy Spirit.

Concerning the first of these questions it should be understood, as said above, that the gifts are given to aid the virtues. These virtues enable the powers of the human soul to be ready to perform

---

* Understood by Jerome as a prophesy of the virgin birth of Christ.

their proper acts, but only in a human mode. For example, faith enables us to see God, but only obscurely as in a mirror. For a virtue may have two sorts of defect; one is accidental and from some lack of proper disposition in the person because of which the virtue remains defective in the person, and this can be removed by growth in the virtue; the other defect, however, is on the part of the virtue itself, for example, as faith is imperfect in the person according to its own disposition, because it is essentially obscure; and this kind of defect can be removed only by a superior virtue given by God, which is called a "gift," since it transcends, as it were, the human mode of operation, for example, the gift of knowledge (*scientia*), which enables one to understand matters of faith surely and clearly.

On the other hand, an act proceeding from a virtue perfected by a gift is called a "beatitude," which is nothing other than an activity according to perfect virtue, as the philosopher says and as is said in Matthew 5:8, *Blessed are the clean of heart, for they shall see God.* Such a perfect activity, however, is accompanied by delight, since delight is the operation of a habit which is unhindered, as the philosopher said, and hence it is called a "fruit." Whence Ambrose commenting on Galatians 5:22, *The fruits of the spirit are love, peace,* etc., says that these acts are called "fruits" inasmuch as they refresh minds with sincere delight.

Concerning the second question, the number of the gifts of the Holy Spirit can be taken in three ways: Since the gifts are perfected either through avoidance of evil, and this is by the gift of *fear of the Lord,* or through access to the good, and then either according to the contemplative or the active life.

If the gifts are taken according to the contemplative life, they can be taken either as to contemplation of the goal of all things, and this is the gift of *wisdom,* which is knowledge of the highest causes, or as to contemplation of those things which are means to the goal, and this is *understanding (intellectus,* insight, intuition), which is of spiritual creatures and what pertains to them. If according to the active life, this either regards duties to which all are obliged, and this is carried out by the gift of piety (which is reverence toward those who by faith or example are witnesses of God) and is guided by the gift of *knowledge* (*scientia*); or it regards duties to which not all are obliged, and to this pertains the gift of *fortitude* (for exposure to difficulties) and is guided by the gift of *counsel*.

Concerning the third question, how the gifts are ordered, it is clear from all this that the gifts are ordered according to their perfection, and this order is to be taken from what they give, not from what is received. It is obvious that wisdom gives order to or regulates understanding (*intellectus*), since it pertains to the wise to order matters; and that the sciences are regulated by the supreme science, namely, metaphysics. It is also clear that counsel regulates fortitude, that knowledge (*scientia*) regulates piety, and that fear regulates all these matters, since it deals with avoidance of all the evils contrary to the goods which the others govern.

Concerning the fourth question of how Christ possesses these gifts, it must be understood that Christ has these gifts according to their most excellent use, as they will be used in heaven. For he does not have servile fear that he should fear punishment, or even filial fear that he should fear he might sin; but only that chaste fear which is reverence (as Hebrews 5:7 says, *He was heard because of his reverence* [*eulabeia*, a synonym for *eusebeia*] *to the Father*). And likewise it is evident as regards the other gifts. It is said of Christ specifically, however, that he is *filled* with the gift of fear, lest it be believed from the greatness of his gifts that he was proud, as was the highest angel, Lucifer, of whom Exodus 28:17 says, *You became haughty of heart because of your beauty, for the sake of splendor you debased your wisdom*; or because Christ came to save us through his humility (Matthew 11:29, *Learn of me for I am meek and humble of heart*).

Concerning the fifth point, it must be understood that if these gifts are considered according to their specific essences, for example, knowledge precisely as knowledge, then those which perfect the intelligence should be appropriated to the Son, and those which pertain to the affective life, to the Holy Spirit, although all are gifts of the whole Trinity. If, however, they are considered generically as gifts, all are attributed to the Holy Spirit, who is the first gift, in whom all other gifts are given. Likewise, if they are also considered as to the principal motive for which they are given, this is love. For the goodness of God, as says [Pseudo-]Dionysius, is diffusive of all that is received from God in created beings, and this divine goodness is appropriated to the Holy Spirit.

Prayer in the Holy Spirit

As a Dominican friar Thomas chanted the psalms and began a commentary on them, but was able to complete only the first fifty-four psalms. While in the *Summa Theologiae* II-II, qq. 83-85, he wrote an extensive treatise on prayer, adoration and sacrifice, in this psalm commentary we see his own daily meditations. Of course, he used the Vulgate Latin psalms, but scholar that he was he also consulted the version Jerome made directly from the Hebrew and the *Gloss*, an important medieval commentary, as well as the comments of the Church Fathers, especially Augustine and Gregory the Great.

In his Prologue Thomas explains the Christian significance and use of the psalms. In his view they refer prophetically to Christ even in their literal sense, which he argued must be the basis of all theological argument. Modern biblical scholarship would hesitate to go so far but would admit that at least some of the psalms are messianic. As the *General Instruction on the Liturgy of the Hours*, printed in the Roman Breviary, says (n. 109):

> The Fathers of the Church saw the whole psalter as a prophecy of Christ, and the Church explained it in this sense; for the same reason the psalms have been chosen for us in the sacred liturgy. . . . [The Fathers] and the sacred liturgy itself could legitimately hear in the singing of the psalms the voice of Christ crying out to the Father, or of the Father conversing with the Son; indeed, they also

recognized in the psalms the voice of the Church, the apostles and the martyrs. . . . A christological meaning is by no means confined to the recognized messianic psalms but is given also to many others. Some of these interpretations are doubtless christological only in an accommodated sense, but they have the traditional approval of the Church.

Since Jesus himself recited the psalms, even on the cross (Mk 15:33-34), we certainly can think, feel and pray them with him, as Thomas tried to do.

Commentary on the Psalms of David

Prologue

With his every deed he offered thanks to God Most High, in words of praise. (Sirach 47:8)

The words of this text speak of David. It is quite appropriate that they be taken as showing the reason for this particular work. They show its four causes: its subject matter, its literary form or genre, its end or purpose, and its author.

The subject matter is universal, for while the individual books of the canonical scriptures may have their particular matters to discuss, this book has as a general topic the whole of theology. This is what [Pseudo-]Dionysius says in the third book of the *Celestial Hierarchy:* "To meditate on the sacred writing of the Divine Odes, that is, the psalms, is to sing of all the sacred and divine activities." And so when the text says, *With his every deed,** the subject matter of this book is indicated, since it treats of every work of God. Now the activity of God is fourfold: creation (Genesis 2:2, *God rested on the seventh day from all the work*); government (John 5:17, *My Father is at work until now*); restoration (John 4:34, *My food is to do the will of him who sent me, to bring his work to completion*); and glorification (Sirach 42:16, *God's work is full of his glory*).

All of these holy works of God are fully treated in the teaching of this book. First, with regard to the work of creation, Psalm 8:4 says, *I will behold your heavens, the work of your fingers.* Second, regarding government, all the historical parts of the Old Testament are touched upon in this book (Psalm 78:2 says, *I will open my mouth in story*). Third, restoration, both with regard to the head, who is Christ, and with regard to all the effects of grace (Psalm 3:6 says, *Whenever I lay down and slept, the Lord preserved me to rise*

---

* The Latin is ambiguous and "his" can refer not to David's but to God's deeds.

again). Everything which pertains to faith in the incarnation is so clearly treated in this work that it almost seems to be a gospel, rather than prophecy. Fourth, there is the work of glorification (Psalm 149:5 says, *The saints will exult in glory*).

The reason why the Church makes such great use of the psalter is that it contains all of scripture, or as the *Gloss* says, it gives us hope for the divine mercy since, even though David sinned, he was restored through repentance. The subject matter of the psalms is therefore truly universal, since it treats of every work of God. It thus looks toward Christ in whom *all the fullness of divinity was pleased to dwell* (Col 1:19). And so the matter of this book is Christ and his members.

There are many different types of literary genre or form to be found in sacred scripture. *Narrative:* Sirach 42:17, *Has not God made his saints tell of all his wonderful deeds?* which is to be found in the historical books; *admonition, exhortation, commands:* Titus 2:15, *Say these things, exhort, and correct with authority,* 2 Timothy 2:14, *Remind people of these things and charge them before God to stop disputing about words,* a genre found in the law, the prophets, and the books of Solomon; *disputation,* as in Job and the Apostle Paul: Job 13:3, *I wish to reason with God;* and the *deprecatory* or *laudatory* genre, and this is what is found in this book.

Whatever is found in the other books in the genres already mentioned is found here by way of praise and prayer (as Psalm 9:2 says, *I will praise you, Lord with all my heart, I will declare all your wondrous deeds*). This text, Sirach 47:8, reads in words of praise, because the psalmist speaks in the laudatory genre. This explains the inscription of this book:* *Here begins the book of hymns or soliloquies of the prophet David concerning Christ.* A hymn is praise of God in song, and song is an exultation of mind about everlasting things which breaks forth in vocal expression. Thus, David teaches us to praise God with exultation, sometimes in a soliloquy, that is, a conversation of an individual person with God or only with himself, as would be appropriate in praising or praying.

---

* In the medieval editions.

The end or purpose of this part of scripture is prayer, the lifting up of the mind to God. According to John Damascene in his *The Orthodox Faith III*, "Prayer is the ascent of the intellect to God." Psalm 141:2 says, *Let my prayer be incense before you, my uplifted hands an evening sacrifice,* and there are four ways in which the soul is lifted up to God. First, by admiring the loftiness of his power (Isaiah 40:26, *Lift up your eyes on high and see who has created these things;* Psalm 104:24, *How wonderful are your works, O Lord*), a lifting up in faith. Second, the mind is lifted up when it looks toward the excellence of eternal happiness (Job 11:15-17, *Surely then you may lift up your face in innocence; you may stand firm and unafraid. For then you shall forget your misery, or recall it like waters that have ebbed away*), a lifting up that comes from hope. Third, the mind is lifted up when it clings to the divine goodness and holiness (Isaiah 51:17, *Awake, awake! Arise O Jerusalem, You who once drank at the Lord's hand the cup of his wrath*), the lifting up that comes from love. Fourth, the mind is lifted up when it imitates the divine justice at work (Lamentations 3:41, *Let us search and examine our ways that we may return to the Lord! Let us reach out our hearts toward God in heaven!*), a lifting up that comes from justice.

These four ways are implied in the text when it says, *to God Most High*. The latter two pertain to the word *God*, the Holy One; the first two to the word *Most High*. That this is the purpose of this book of the Bible is to be found in the psalms themselves. First, with regard to the words *Most High*, we read in Psalm 113:3-4, *From the rising of the sun to its setting, let the name of the Lord be praised. High above the heavens is the Lord, above the heavens, God's glory*. Then, with regard to the word *God* we read in Psalm 99:3, *Let them praise your great and awesome name, holy is God!*

Thus, Gregory the Great says in his *Homilies on Ezekiel*, n. 1, that when psalmody is carried out with the attention of the heart it prepares a way to the heart for almighty God. He can then infuse into the attentive soul either the mysteries of prophecy or the grace of compunction. The purpose of the Book of Psalms, therefore, is that the soul be joined to God as the All Holy and Most High.

The author of this work is indicated by the text in the phrase *in words of praise*. Note that authorship of sacred scripture is different from authorship of works on other subjects. Other forms of knowledge are works of human reason, but the scriptures are a work of divine inspiration (2 Peter 1:20-21 says, *Know this first of all, that there is no prophecy of scripture that is a matter of personal interpretation, for no prophecy ever came through human will, but rather human beings moved by the Holy Spirit spoke under the influence of God*). Thus, in sacred scripture, the tongue of the human being functions like the tongue of a boy who says words which someone else furnishes (Psalm 45:2 says, *My tongue is the pen of a nimble scribe*, and in 2 Samuel 23:2 David says, *The spirit of the Lord spoke through me, his word was on my tongue*).

And so the text says *in words of praise*, which are said by means of revelation (1 Kings 20:35 relates how a guild prophet was compelled by the Lord to demand his own punishment by saying, *Strike me!* that is, by divine revelation). This biblical Book of Psalms can be called *a word of praise* in four ways, because it is related to glory in four ways. First, it is related as to the cause from which it flows, because this teaching arises from the praise or glory which God himself bestows (2 Peter 1:17-18 says, *For he received honor and glory from God the Father when that unique declaration came to him from the majestic glory, "This is my Son, my beloved, with whom I am well pleased." We ourselves heard this voice come from heaven while we were with him on the holy mountain*). Second, this book is related to praise as containing it, because this book contains the glory and praise of God which it proclaims (as Psalm 96:3 says, *Tell God's glory among the nations*). Third, it is related to glory or praise with regard to the way it shines forth from God. Glory is the same thing as splendor, and the revelation of this prophecy was glorious because it took place in a splendid manner.

There are, indeed, three modes of prophecy: through sensible things (Daniel 5:5 relates how at the feast of Belshazzar, *Suddenly, opposite the lampstand, the fingers of a human hand appeared, writing on the plaster of the wall in the king's palace. When the king saw the hand that wrote his face blanched*); or through imaginary likenesses (such as is evident in Genesis 41 in the dream of Pharaoh and Joseph's interpretation of it, and also in Isaiah 6:1, *I saw the Lord sitting upon a high and lofty throne*); or through a manifestation of the truth itself. This last mode of prophecy was characteristic of David; he set forth his prophecy without any exterior support and under the impulse of the Holy Spirit alone. For the other prophets, as Augustine says, prophesied deeds and sayings by means of certain images of things and a clothing of words, that is, by means of dreams and visions; but this prophet was taught the truth openly.

When David said in 2 Samuel 23:2, *The spirit spoke through me, his word was on my tongue*, he immediately added in verse 4 that God *is like the morning light in sunrise on a cloudless morning*. The sun is the Holy Spirit illuminating the hearts of the prophets. Sometimes he appears behind clouds, as when he shines upon the prophets in the two modes previously mentioned; but sometimes there are no clouds, as is the case here in the psalms. In this regard, one can make reference to the scornful words of Michal to David when he danced, girt only with a linen apron, *leaping and dancing before the Lord*, that is, before the Ark (2 Samuel 6:16, *How the King of Israel has honored himself today, exposing himself to the view of the slave girls of his followers, as a commoner might do!*)

Finally, the psalms are *words of praise* because they invite us to the glory of the heavenly choir praising God (as it says in Psalm 149:5, *Let the faithful rejoice in their glory, cry out for joy at their banquet*, and in verse 9, *Such is the glory of the saints*).

Thus it is clear what the four causes of this work are: its matter concerns all the works of God; its genre is deprecatory or laudatory; its purpose is to join those who have been exalted to union with the Most High and Holy One; the author is the Holy Spirit himself revealing all these things.

Yet, before we get to the actual text of the psalms, we need to consider . . . how they should be interpreted. In reading the psalter, as well as the other prophets, we need above all to avoid one error which was condemned by the Fifth Ecumenical Council of the Church in 553. Theodore of Mopsuestia said that in sacred scripture and the prophets nothing is said explicitly about Christ; rather, these books really speak of certain other matters, which statements have only been accommodated to refer to Christ, for example, Psalm 22:19, *They divided my garments among them,* refers only to David and is not about Christ. But this manner of interpretation was condemned at that council, so that whoever asserts that the scriptures are to be interpreted in that way is a heretic.

Therefore, in writing about Ezekiel, Blessed Jerome handed on to us a rule that we will observe in the psalms: The things related are to be interpreted as prefiguring something about Christ or the Church. As 1 Corinthians 10:11 says, *These things happened as examples for us.* Prophecies were, of course, sometimes pronounced about things of that time, but they were not said principally about them, except insofar as they were a prefigurement of future things. The Holy Spirit ordained that when such things were spoken of, certain things were included that surpassed the condition of the event; that way the soul would be lifted up to what was being prefigured.

Thus, in the Book of Daniel many things are said of King Antiochus IV Epiphanes as a figure of the Antichrist. We read there of certain things which were not fulfilled in Antiochus but will be fulfilled in the Antichrist. So also we read certain things about the reign of David and Solomon which were not to be fulfilled in the reigns of such kings but were to be fulfilled in the reign of Christ. These things were said as a figure of Christ (although Psalm 72, for example, has in its title *of Solomon*), since the Holy Spirit also puts in that psalm certain things which exceed the capability even of such a king; for example, in verse 5:7, *May he live as long as the sun endures, like the moon, through all generations . . . that abundance may flourish in his days, till the moon be no more,* and in verse 8, *May he rule from sea to sea, from the river to the ends of the earth.* Thus, Psalm 72 is to be interpreted as being about the reign of Solomon insofar as it is a figure of the reign of Christ; in that reign all the things that the psalm says will be fulfilled.*

---

* A section giving the division of the whole Psalter is omitted.

Psalm 45

Because Aquinas' commentary is written as very concise notes, we have decided to make the following translation rather free and paraphrastic to make it more accessible to the modern reader. We also have inserted the translation of the New American Bible (NAB) and where possible adapted the commentary to it. Where the divergence was too great we have noted the Latin reading. In this book there is room for the commentary on only one psalm, and we have chosen Psalm 45 as especially relevant to Thomas' spirituality. Apparently Thomas wrote a brief commentary on the Song of Songs, perhaps on his deathbed, but the one that has come down to us under his name seems spurious. Because Psalm 45 is closely related to the Song, it gives us a good idea of how Aquinas might have treated that work. Like John of the Cross, Aquinas understood the Song as a mystical colloquy between Christ, the Bridegroom, and the Church, his Bride (typified in the Blessed Virgin Mary), and therefore between Christ and the individual Christian in prayer.

I

¹ [Title omitted]

² My heart is stirred by a noble theme,
   as I sing my ode to the king.
   My tongue is the pen of a nimble scribe.

II

³ You are the most handsome of men;
   fair speech has graced your lips,
   for God has blessed you forever.

⁴ Gird your sword upon your hip, mighty warrior!
   In splendor and majesty ride on in triumph!

⁵ In the cause of truth and justice
   may your right hand show you wondrous deeds.

⁶ Your arrows are sharp;
   peoples will cower at your feet;
   the king's enemies will lose heart.

⁷ Your throne, O God, stands forever;
   your royal scepter is a scepter for justice.

⁸ You love justice and hate wrongdoing;
    therefore God, your God has anointed you
    with the oil of gladness above your fellow kings.

⁹ With myrrh, aloes, and cassia
    your robes are fragrant.
    From ivory-paneled palaces
    stringed instruments bring you joy.

¹⁰ Daughters of kings are your lovely wives;
    a princess arrayed in Ophir's gold
    comes to stand at your right hand.

III

¹¹ Listen my daughter, and understand;
    pay me careful heed.
    Forget your people and your father's house,

¹² that the king might desire your beauty,
    He is your lord;

¹³ honor him, daughter of Tyre.
    Then the richest of the people
    will seek your favor with gifts.

¹⁴ All glorious is the king's daughter as she enters,
    her raiment threaded with gold;

¹⁵ In embroidered apparel she is led to the king.
    The maids of her train are presented to the king.

¹⁶ They are led in with glad and joyous acclaim;
    they enter the palace of the king.

IV

¹⁷ The throne of your fathers your sons will have;
    you shall make them princes through all the land.

¹⁸ I will make your name renowned through all
    generations;
    thus nations shall praise you forever.

Introduction

The first verses of this psalm prompted Thomas to meditate on the inspiration of the Bible. In line with his whole philosophy of God as the First Cause of all being and all truth, for Thomas biblical inspiration is not an isolated phenomenon but an instance of God's constant self-revelation through the Holy Spirit. As principal author of the Bible, God used as instruments the many human authors to write the various parts of the Bible. Yet, God did not use them as mere mechanical tools, but in such a way as not to deprive them of their own human freedom but to free them to enter into God's own thought and express it appropriately. Likewise God's profound influence in our lives rather than taking away our freedom makes us free.

The psalmist in Psalm 44 has just prayed for the kingdom and the king in time of trouble; now he seems to give thanks for the glory of the king and the kingdom which has resulted from God's favor and he presents the glory of the king and the magnificence of his kingdom. This psalm is called an *epithalamium*, because it was the custom at weddings that certain songs were sung in honor of the bride and groom, and these are called "epithalamic" or nuptial. Thus the subject matter of this psalm is a certain espousal between Christ and the Church, which was begun when the Son of God united himself to a human nature in the womb of the Virgin (as Psalm 19:6 says, *And he comes forth like a bridegroom from his chamber*). Thus the subject matter of this psalm is the same as that of the book of the Bible which is called the Song of Songs.

This psalm is divided into three parts. A preface to the canticle is first set forth in verses 1-2, then praise of the groom in verses 3-10, and finally praise of the bride in verses 11-18. In the preface the psalmist does three things: First, in verse 2a, he speaks of the publication of the psalm; then, in verse 2b, of its purpose; and finally, in verse 2c, of its author. He describes the publication when he says, *My heart is stirred by a noble theme* (Latin: *overflows with a noble theme*), that is, his heart overflows because it is so full or rather overfull; hence he sings from great devotion and wisdom (as Matthew 12:34 says, *For from the fullness of the heart the mouth speaks*). Note that the publication of this psalm is attributed to the heart; it has been composed out of great devotion. The author is not one of those about whom Isaiah 29:13 says, *This people draws near with words only and honors me with their lips alone.* Rather, the psalmist proclaims from his heart the praises of Christ (as 1 Corinthians 14:15b says, *I sing praise with my spirit but I will also sing praise with my mind*). The psalmist's heart *is stirred* by a *noble theme,* that is, by this psalm, which is *noble* because it is encouraging, since it speaks of the mysteries of Christ and the Church (as 1 Timothy 1:15 says, *This saying is trustworthy and deserves full acceptance; Christ Jesus came into the world to save sinners,* and Zechariah 1:13 says, *To the angel who spoke with me, the Lord replied with comforting words*).

In verse 2b the psalmist speaks of the purpose of the psalm when he says, *as I sing my ode to the king,* that is, in honor of the king, who is Christ (as Isaiah 32:1 says, *See, a king will rule justly*), that is, "I sing this song in honor of Christ, to whom we should dedicate all our works" (as Colossians 3:17 says, *Whatever you do in word or in deed, do everything in the name of the Lord Jesus, giving thanks to God the Father through him*).

In verse 2c, *My tongue is the pen of a nimble scribe,* he describes the author of the psalm as a *tongue.* It is as if he is saying, "Do not think that I have done this on my own; it has been done only with the assistance of the Holy Spirit, who uses my tongue the way a writer uses a pen." Thus, the principal author of this psalm is the Holy Spirit (as in 2 Samuel 23:2 David the psalmist says, *The spirit of the Lord spoke through me; his word was on my tongue,* that is, as through an instrument, and 2 Peter 1:20-21 says, *Know this first of all, that there is no prophecy of scripture that is a matter of personal interpretation, for no prophecy ever came through human will, but rather human beings moved by the Holy Spirit spoke under the influence of God*).

Whose pen is it? It is the pen *of a nimble scribe,* that is, the pen of the Holy Spirit, who writes swiftly upon the human heart. Whoever seeks wisdom through his own endeavor studies piecemeal and also over a long period of time, but whoever possesses it from the Holy Spirit receives it swiftly (as Acts of the Apostles 2:2 says of the coming of the Holy Spirit at Pentecost, *Suddenly there came from the sky a noise like a strong driving wind*). Those who possess knowledge by divine revelation are filled with wisdom suddenly, like the apostles who were suddenly filled with the Holy Spirit (as Psalm 147:15 says, *His word runs swiftly*, and Sirach 11:21 says, *Trust in the Lord and wait for his light, for it is easy with the Lord suddenly, in an instant, to make a poor man rich*).

Or the *pen of a nimble scribe* may mean the pen belongs to one who writes quickly (as the Creator works according to Psalm 148:5, *For the Lord commanded and they were created*). But the *tongue* can also refer to something else, because the psalmist did not want merely to speak; rather he first thought this over in his heart, then spoke with his mouth, and finally wrote it all down. In other words, this psalm is meant to profit not only those who are present, who hear it, but also those who are to come (as God said to Isaiah, in 8:1, *Take a large cylinder-seal, and inscribe on it in ordinary letters*, and Habakkuk 2:2 says, *Then the Lord answered me and said: Write down the vision clearly upon tablets, so that one can read it readily*).

However, some exegetes think that these words are spoken in praise of Christ's divinity as if they were words of God the Father. Augustine and Jerome do not approve of this interpretation, but [Pseudo-]Dionysius uses it in the second chapter of *On the Divine Names*, where he quotes this verse. According to this interpretation, Christ is here being praised by the Father in three ways in the three lines of this verse: First, his eternal birth from the Father is described, then his power, and finally his activity.

With regard to Christ's eternal birth from the Father, the psalmist says four things: First, there is his procession by nature, where it says, *My heart is stirred* (*overflows*), indicating a kind of emanation from a fullness; the procession of the Son from the Father is an overflowing, because the Son proceeds from out of the fullness of the divine nature (as John 3:35 says, *The Father loves the Son and has given everything over to him*). Second, he describes the manner of this overflow; the Son does not come forth from the Father in a corporeal way or from some other nature but in a purely spiritual way, that is indicated by *My heart*, that is, the Father's heart, which implies that the Son did not come out of nothing, that is, was not created; nor from some other essence but from God's very being (as Psalm 110:3, Latin, says, *From the womb before the day star I have begotten you*). Third, the Father names the Son who proceeds from him as the *Word* (the *ode* or song) (as John 1:1 says, *In the beginning was the Word*). Finally, he presents the perfection of the one proceeding forth in the phrase *noble theme*, in the sense of having the full goodness of the divinity (as Jesus says in Luke 18:19, *No one is good but God alone*).

The Father shows his power when he says, *I sing my ode*, meaning "I do all my works" *to the king*, that is, in honor of the king, namely, of the Son, who is one God with me (as John 1:3 says, *All things were made through him*). The Son's own activity is indicated when it says, *My tongue is the pen of a nimble scribe*, that is, "My son is my tongue and my pen as nimble scribe." In sacred scripture, the instruments or bodily members that are principles of activities are used as metaphors for the activities themselves. Thus, the tongue and the pen indicate the activity which pertains to a tongue and a pen. The activity of the tongue is to impart to others the wisdom of the heart; the pen indicates that the wisdom which is in the heart is transmitted by a material that can be sensed, namely, parchment.

Now God both speaks and writes. He speaks when he transmits his wisdom to rational minds (as Psalm 85:9 says, *I will listen for the word of God*). What God the Father speaks is called the Word, and all illumination takes place by means of it (as John 1:4 says, *And this life was the light of the human race*). God writes because he imprints the judgments of his wisdom within rational created beings (as Romans 1:20 says, *Ever since the creation of the world, God's invisible attributes of eternal power and divinity have been able to be understood and perceived in what he has made*, and Sirach 1:8 says *He has poured her [wisdom] forth upon all his works*). A person who looks at a book recognizes the wisdom of its author; in the same way, when we see created beings, we recognize the wisdom of God. Thus, the Word of God is a pen.

The Praise of Christ, the Royal Bridegroom

Thomas' christology differs from that of the Franciscan School in that he refrains from speculation as to whether the incarnation would have taken place if there had been no sin. For Aquinas, revelation has told us only that the Word was made flesh for us and our salvation from sin. But granted that fact, the God-Man becomes the goal of the entire universe, and this is the greater good which God has brought about from the ruin caused by angelic and human sin, the *felix culpa*, the "happy fault." Our return to God, therefore, can only be through incorporation in Christ, and our prayer must always be made in and through him to the Father by the inspiration of the Holy Spirit. Hans Urs van Balthasar has pointed out how often theologians have spoken of the truth and goodness of God but neglected his "glory" or beauty. Here is one place that Aquinas meditates on this theme.

In verse 4 we read, *You are the most handsome of men.* What has gone before was according to one interpretation the prologue or according to the other interpretation the praise of Christ's divinity. The psalmist now presents the praise of Christ in his humanity, and because he said, *I sing my ode to the king,* he praises Christ under the metaphor of a king, namely David, on the grounds of four qualities: in verse 3, his graciousness; in verses 4-6, his military prowess; in verse 7, his authority as a judge; and in verse 8, his pleasures. With regard to the first of these he makes two remarks: First, in verse 3a, he describes the king's graciousness; then, in verse 3b, its cause or effect.

Note that in a human being there are two senses which are particularly active, namely, sight and hearing. It is, therefore, through these two that a person appears gracious: because of beauty that appeals to the sense of sight and because of gracious words that appeal to the sense of hearing. Now these two were found supremely in Christ (as the bridegroom says of the bride in Song of Songs 2:14, *Let me see you, let me hear your voice, for your voice is sweet, and you are lovely*). Christ, the bridegroom, is himself handsome and eloquent in the ways which befitted what he had to communicate. With regard to the former the psalmist says, *You are the most handsome of men.*

In Christ there was a fourfold beauty. One was in terms of his divine form (Philippians 2:6 says, *though he was in the form of God*), and in this he was infinitely more beautiful than any human being. All created beings have grace by an overflow and participation in the divine beauty, while God the Son has it by his very nature and in its fullness (Colossians 2:9 says, *For in him dwells the whole fullness of the deity bodily*, and Hebrews 1:3 says of Jesus, *He who is the refulgence of his [God's] glory, the very imprint of his being*, and Wisdom 7:26 says, *For she [wisdom] is the refulgence of eternal light, the spotless mirror of the power of God, the image of his goodness*).

A second type of beauty is that of justice and truth (Jeremiah 31:23, Vulgate, says, *May the Lord bless you, the beauty of justice*, and John 1:14 says, *We saw his glory, the glory of the Father's Son, full of grace and truth*).

A third type of beauty is that of honorable conduct (as 1 Peter 5:3 says, a presbyter should be *an example to the flock*). In this regard Jesus was the most handsome among men, because his conduct was more honorable and virtuous than that of any other (as 1 Peter 2:22 says, quoting Isaiah 53:9, *He committed no sin; no deceit was found in his mouth*). Augustine says, "To us who know him, he is handsome in every way: beautiful in the arms of his parents, beautiful in his miracles, beautiful in his scourging, beautiful in laying down his life, beautiful on the gibbet, beautiful on the wood of the cross, beautiful in heaven."

The fourth type of beauty is that of the body, and even this is to be found in Christ (in Song of Songs 1:16 the bride says to the bridegroom, *Ah, you are beautiful, my lover!*). Yet is it really true that in bodily appearance Jesus was *the most handsome of men?* It seems not, because Isaiah 53:2 says of the Messiah, *He grew up like a sapling before him [God], like a shoot from the parched earth. There was in him no stately bearing to make us look at him, nor appearance that would attract us to him. He was spurned and avoided by men, a man of suffering, accustomed to infirmity, one of those from whom men hide their faces, spurned, and we held him in no esteem.* This can also be shown to be reasonable: Christ wanted to be poor and not use riches in order to teach us to hold them in contempt; but just as these things are to be held in contempt, so too is bodily beauty (Proverbs 31:30 says, *Charm is deceptive, and beauty fleeting*).

My response to this difficulty is that beauty, health, and other things of this sort are to be valued in relation to something greater. A certain balance of bodily humors that is healthy in a boy is not necessarily so in an old man; what is healthy for a lion might be death for a human being. In short, health is the right balance of humors for a specific nature. In a similar way, beauty consists in a proper proportion of shapes and colors. Thus, the beauty of one thing occurs in one way, that of another thing in a different way. And so Christ had a bodily beauty that was appropriate to the status and dignity of his condition. Therefore, one should not think that Christ had flaxen hair or a fair complexion because this would have been unbecoming for him. But he did have to the highest degree the kind of bodily beauty which was relevant to his status, dignity, and graciousness of appearance. As Augustine says, his face radiated a certain divine quality such that everyone revered him.

To the first objection, I would reply that the prophet Isaiah wanted to express the contempt which Christ suffered in his passion when his bodily appearance was disfigured because of the multitude of his afflictions. To the other objection, I would say that the riches and beauty we should hold in contempt are the ones which we are tempted to use badly.

Jesus was also gracious in his words, and so the psalmist says, *Fair speech has graced your lips* (as Sirach 6:5 says, *A kind mouth multiplies friends, and gracious lips prompt friendly greetings*). There are three reasons why a person's words are considered gracious. The first is because a person says things pleasant and useful, and the words of Christ were gracious in this way because he placed only light demands upon us and promised us rest (Matthew 11:28 says, *Come to me all you who labor and are burdened, and I will give you rest*, and the apostles say to him, in John 6:68, *Master, to whom shall we go? You have the words of eternal life*).

Someone is also said to have gracious words on account of the orderly and moving way he has of speaking and this was the way Jesus spoke (as Psalm 119:140 says, *Your servant loves your promise, it has been proved by fire*). Again, one has gracious words because of his ability to persuade others, and Christ had this gift also (Matthew 7:29 and 21:23 says that he was teaching in the temple, *as one having authority*. Because of this, Luke 21:38 says, *All the people would get up early each morning to listen to him in the temple area*, and in John 7:46 even the temple guards reported to the High Priest that *Never before has anyone spoken like this one*).

When in verse 3c the psalmist says, *For God has blessed you forever*, he presents either the cause or the effect of these qualities of Christ. As has been said, being blessed by God designates either an effect of someone's goodness or its cause, that is, God's favor. Now God bestowed a twofold favor on the man Christ: glory and kingship. These were rewards for Christ's merits (Philippians 2:9 says, *And therefore God has exalted him*), since the word *for* means *therefore* and indicates that these merits have brought it about, that is "Because you are handsome of form and gracious in your teaching, therefore, *God has blessed you forever* with the blessing of a spiritual kingdom."

Another way to understand this is as a cause of the favor of grace, and then the meaning is that *God has blessed you forever* for this purpose: that you might be handsome and gracious of speech.

In verse 4 with *Gird your sword upon your hip, mighty warrior!* the psalmist begins to describe Christ as powerful in virtue. First, in verse 4a, his military virtue is presented; then, in verse 4b, the way he goes into battle; and finally, in verse 5, the effect of his fighting. Military virtue consists in natural bravery and the proper preparation of weapons; but the psalmist mentions first the preparation of weapons when he says, *Gird your sword* and then adds, *upon your hip, mighty warrior!* thereby indicating the might of his weapons (as Song of Songs 3:8 says, *The valiant men of Israel, all of them expert with the sword, skilled in battle, each with his sword at his side against danger in the watches of the night*).

Now according to the *Gloss*, it is one thing *to gird your sword upon your hip* in readiness for battle, as soldiers do (as Judas

Maccabaeus in 1 Maccabees 3:58-59 says, *Arm yourselves and be brave, in the morning be ready to fight these Gentiles who have assembled against us to destroy our sanctuary. It is better for us to die than to witness the ruin of our nation and our sanctuary. Whatever heaven wills, he will do*); but it is quite another thing to put on an apron in readiness to serve others (Jesus says in Luke 12:37 of the Messiah *He will gird himself, have them [his servants, the apostles] recline at table and proceed to wait on them*). It is still another thing to be girded in readiness to go on a journey (Sirach 36:26 speaks of *armed bands*, guerrillas that wander from city to city), and it is still another to be ungirded as those who are ready to rest (as the king of Israel says to the king of Aram in 1 Kings 20:11, *It is not for a man who is buckling his armor to boast as if he were taking it off*).

The sword of Christ, however, is his teaching. Ephesians 6:17 speaks of this sword as *the sword of the Spirit, which is the word of God*. With this sword Christ creates division in this world to distinguish the good from the wicked (Matthew 10:34 says, *I have come to bring not peace but the sword*). This sword is sharp on both sides (as John's vision of Christ testifies in Revelation 1:15, *A sharp two-edged sword came out of his mouth*), because it instructs us both about eternal and about temporal matters.

Furthermore, Christ's sword is *upon your [his] hip*, because he employed the instrument of his humanity for the words of his teaching (Isaiah 52:6 says, *Therefore on that day my people shall know my renown, that it is I who have foretold it. Here I am!*). When the psalmist says *mighty warrior!* he shows the strength or power which is natural to Christ (1 Samuel 2:2b says, *There is no rock like our God*, and Job 9:19 says, *If it be a question of strength, he is mighty, and if of judgment who will call him to account?*).

According to Jerome and the Hebrew text the phrase, *In splendor and majesty* in verse 4b should be joined with the preceding *mighty warrior!* as one verse, and it is read in the same way in the *Gloss*. The meaning then is: You, O Christ, are the most powerful one, not only in your outward appearance as warrior, that is, in your humanity, but also in your divine splendor and majesty, that is, in your divinity.

In terms of his humanity, he is also the greatest in strength among men (Song of Songs 5:15 says of the bridegroom, *His stature is like the trees of Lebanon, imposing as the cedars,* and as for his beauty, Wisdom 13:3 says to the worshipers of the sun and moon, *Now if out of joy in their beauty they thought them gods, let them know how far more excellent is the Lord than these; for the original source of beauty fashioned them*). Or perhaps the meaning of this verse is that Christ, because he is most powerful, is splendid in beauty; hence Jerome adds the phrase *to your praise,* that is, the reason why you are praiseworthy and glorious is that you are armed and strong.

Next, in verse 4b, we read *Ride on in triumph!* In praise of Christ, the psalmist has just presented the courage and splendor of a king, but now he deals with the king's riding forth, and deals with two things: first, in verse 4b, with this riding forth; and then, in verse 5, with its purpose. With regard to the former, note that the Vulgate has three phrases: *Set your course, proceed prosperously, and reign,* while Jerome's translation from the Hebrew has only one: *Ride on triumphant!* (as Jeremiah 49:19 says, *As when a lion comes up from the thicket of Jordan*).

It is clear that these three phrases in the Latin text pertain to a certain completion of this marching forth. In marching to war there are three things to be considered: the starting point, the middle of the march, and its destination. The starting point ought to be a careful and prudent stocktaking of what is involved (Proverbs 24:6 says, *For it is by wise guidance that you wage your war, and the victory is due to a wealth of counselors,* and Luke 14:31 says, *What king marching into battle would not first sit down and decide whether with ten thousand troops he can successfully oppose another king advancing upon him with twenty thousand?*). *Set your course* means consider carefully, but for Christ setting the course indicates his compassionate purpose of mercy, that is, the salvation of the human race (Psalm 38:23 says, *Come quickly to help me, my Lord and my salvation!*).

The middle of this march should be well executed. But there are two ways in which Christ can be said to march forth. One way is by coming forth from the womb of the Virgin at his nativity (in the words of Psalm 19:6, *He comes forth like a bridegroom from his chamber*), and this coming forth was well executed, because he was born without sin, and moreover he did not deprive his mother of her virginity nor occasion her any pain. In another way, Christ traveled far and wide from one person to another to convert them, and this journey prospered, because in the end it will achieve the conversion of the whole world (as Isaiah 55:11 says, *So shall my word be that goes forth from my mouth; It shall not return to me void, but shall do my will, achieving the end for which I sent it*, and Psalm 118:25 says, *Lord grant salvation! Lord grant good fortune!*).

Yet the phrase Set your course can also be combined with the terms *splendor* and *majesty* so as to say in effect, "Set your course by means of the splendid power of your humanity and the hidden beauty of your divinity."

The destination of this march forth is to establish his kingdom (Psalm 47:9 says, *God rules over the nations; God sits upon his holy throne*), thus Christ's goal is to reign in the hearts of all through faith (as Gabriel says to Mary in Luke 1:32, *He will reign over the house of Jacob forever*). And this is why the psalmist concludes with *triumphant!* as the purpose of Christ's marching forth, and continues in verse 5, *In the cause of truth and justice*. Thus the end of his marching forth is in the *cause of truth*, but this can refer either to the dispositive cause of his going forth or to its final cause.

Let us first take it as indicating a dispositive cause and consider the text as Jerome translates it: *because of the word of truth and the meekness of justice*. There are two things that are necessary for a king to act successfully. The first is to be believed by others, since if nothing he says is believed, yet he himself believes others, he cannot be a leader (Proverbs 17:7 says, *Fine words are out of place in a fool; how much more, lying words in a noble!*).

The second thing a king needs is to be loved by his people. If he is not loved, he cannot prosper in his kingdom or in his dealings. The meekness and clemency of the king is what makes him loved. (Sirach 3:17 says, *My son, conduct yourself with humility, and you will be loved more than a giver of gifts*). Thus, these two things predispose for the prosperity of the kingdom (as Proverbs 20:28 says, *Kindness and piety safeguard the king, and he upholds his throne by justice,* and Psalm 37:11 says, *But the poor* [Latin: *meek*] *will possess the land, and delight in great prosperity*).

But according to our Latin text, in order for the king to prosper in his dealings, there are three things that he ought to have: truth, meekness, and justice. These three things made Christ prosper, because he was truthful in teaching, meek in suffering, and just in acting. As to the first, Matthew 22:16 says of Christ, *Teacher, we know that you are a truthful man and that you teach the way of God in accordance with the truth.* As to the second, 1 Peter 2:23 says, *When he was insulted, he returned no insult; when he suffered, he did not threaten,* and Jeremiah 11:19, *Yes I, like a trusting lamb led to slaughter, had not realized that they were hatching plots against me.* As to the third, Christ in no way deviated from justice; as Psalm 145:17 says, *You, Lord, are just in all your ways, faithful in all your works.*

On the other hand, if this *in the cause of* [or Latin: *because of*] indicates Christ's purpose, then the sense is: *Set your course, proceed prosperously, and reign* in order to do the *truth.* Now Christ did the truth in two ways: by fulfilling the promises and by accomplishing what was prefigured (Romans 15:8 says, *Christ became a minister of the circumcised to show God's truthfulness, to confirm the promises to the patriarchs,* and 2 Corinthians 1:20 says, *For however many are the promises of God their Yes is in him*). Also he should reign for the sake of the humility which he wished to teach his disciples (as Jesus says in Matthew 11:29, *Learn from me, for I am meek and humble of heart*). He is to *reign* also for the sake of justice (as John 5:22 says, *Nor does the Father judge anyone, but he gives all judgment to the Son*).

In verse 5b we read, *May your right hand show you wondrous deeds.* This indicates a very specific manner of marching forth: *Proceed prosperously.* In what manner? *May your right hand show you wondrous deeds.* In a warlike metaphor, the psalmist says that, if you face an enemy, it is only fitting that your hand holding a weapon should clear a path for you, and that you should go toward your foe in this way into battle, that is, proceed as your right hand clears a path for you. And this will happen wondrously, because all will be amazed at your victory. Jerome has: *Your right hand will bring you out*, that is, since you will do glorious things, your hand will show how wonderful you are.

Yet in Psalm 138:7 Christ says to God the Father, *You stretch out your hand; your right hand saves me;* but I would say that this phrase is not contrary to the other, because Christ is both God and man. Insofar as he is God, his right hand is the same as that of the Father (as Exodus 15:6 says, *Your right hand, O Lord, magnificent in power, your right hand, O Lord, has shattered the enemy*), yet as human, Jesus' own right hand leads him forth wondrously in the attack against his enemies. The same is true when Jesus works miracles by virtue of his divinity, yet also by the touch of his hand.

Christ has thus prepared a way for himself into the human heart (Psalm 118:16 says, *The Lord's right hand is raised; the Lord's right hand strikes with power*). If we consider Christ's way of acting, it is indeed wonderful (as Esther says in Esther D:14, Latin 15:17, to the King of Persia, *For you are awesome, my Lord, though your glance is full of kindness*, and Psalm 139:14 says, *Wonderful are your works*).

Next, in verse 6, we read, *Your arrows are sharp*, that is, you have made a way for yourself, because your arrows are sharp. Here the psalmist describes the power and effect of Christ's weapons, that is, the arrows of his words, called arrows for three reasons. First, because an arrow has a sharp point and can penetrate to the heart (God says of Israel in Hosea 2:16, *I will lead her into the desert and speak to her heart*). Such were the words of Christ (as Hebrews 4:12 says, *The word of God is living and effective, sharper than any two-edge sword, penetrating between soul and spirit, joints and marrow, and able to discern reflections and thoughts of the heart*). Furthermore, an arrow moves swiftly (in Wisdom 5:12, the passing of life is described as an arrow).

Similarly, the words of Christ filled the whole world suddenly, because Christ's word had spread through almost the whole world before the destruction of Jerusalem (Psalm 147:15 says, *His word runs swiftly*). Finally, an arrow reaches to remote places, and so did Christ's word (Psalm 19:5 says, *Their report goes forth through all the earth, their message, to the ends of the world*). Similarly, the word of God is a sword, insofar as it wounded the Jews; they were converted to Christ as to someone close at hand. But it is also an arrow insofar as it reached the distant Gentiles, and they were converted to Christ (Ephesians 2:17 says, *He came and preached peace to you who were far off and peace to those who were near*).

Next, in verse 6b, the psalmist writes, *Peoples will cower at your feet*, and describes the effect of the divine word, the conversion of people to God; since this means that all will run to Christ (Philippians 2:10 says, *At the name of Jesus every knee should bend*). But what is the meaning of the phrase the psalmist adds in verse 6c, *The king's enemies will lose heart?* This can be understood in two ways. One way is to join it with the first phrase of this verse, as if *peoples will cower at your feet* were interposed. Then the meaning is: Your sharp arrows enter into the hearts of the king's enemies— that is, your words are like arrows which penetrate to the heart, and because of this, peoples will cower at your feet.

Another way to understand *The king's enemies will lose heart* is to join it with the phrase *Peoples will cower at your feet*, so that this subjection takes place in the hearts or rather in the heart of your— the king's—enemies. Now certain people are made subject by coercion, as enemies are subjugated; but the psalmist says that he is speaking not of this kind of subjection but of the voluntary sort. This is why he says, *The king's enemies will lose heart*, that is, they cease to resist and are made subject in their very hearts, though they used to be at heart enemies of Christ (as Psalm 54:8 says, *Then I will offer you generous sacrifice*).

Or to put it another way: *Your arrows are sharp;* the peoples who were enemies of the king, that is, of Christ, are now subject to him; and this is literally what has happened: The Gentiles, who tried to destroy faith in Christ, now serve Christ (as Isaiah 55:5 says, *So you shall summon a nation you knew not, and nations that knew you not shall run to you,* and Psalm 18:44 says, *A people I had not known became my slaves*).

Next, in verse 7-8, the psalmist, who has just praised Christ for his graciousness and his military virtue, now praises him for his authority as a judge. First, in 7a he describes his judicial authority, then, in 7b-8a, the execution of that authority and finally, in 7b, the reason for it.

Thus he says in 7a, *Your throne, O God stands forever.* He says, *Your throne, O God,* because in scripture, judicial authority is symbolized by a throne (as Psalm 122:5 says, *Here are the thrones of justice, the thrones of the house of David*). Now judicial authority befits or, rather, belongs to Christ (as John 5:22 says, *Nor does the Father judge anyone, but he has given all judgment to the Son*). Thus, by the throne of Christ his authority is indicated (as Jesus says to the apostles in Matthew 19:28, *Amen, I say to you that you who have followed me, in the new age, when the Son of Man is seated on his throne of glory will yourselves sit on twelve thrones, judging the twelve tribes of Israel*).

Bishops and kings also have this judicial authority but only as ministers of Christ (as Wisdom 6:4 says, *Though you were ministers of his kingdom, you did not judge rightly*). On the other hand, Christ has this authority as the principal judge and as truly God. Thus, he says, *Your throne, O God,* because God says in Hebrews 10:30, *Vengeance is mine, I will repay.* Here the psalmist is clearly speaking about Christ, since he is directing his remarks to him (thus in Revelation 3:21 Christ says, *I will give the victor the right to sit on my throne, as I myself first won the victory and sit with my Father on his throne,* and Isaiah 6:1 says, *I saw the Lord seated upon a high and lofty throne*).

Furthermore, temporary authority as a judge is one thing, perpetual authority is another—and such is the authority of the Son of God. Thus, the psalmist says, *Your throne . . . stands forever,* because his judgment is for eternity (as Daniel 7:14 says, *His dominion is an everlasting dominion*), for this is how he distinguishes the authority, dignity, and eternity of God.

Then, in verse 7b, the psalmist goes on to deal with the execution of this authority, as he says, *Your royal scepter is a scepter for justice.* First he sets forth the execution of Christ's authority, then he explains it. Now it is necessary for a king to restrain crime. As Aristotle says, if human souls were so well ordered by God that they would obey paternal warnings, kings and judges would not be necessary. But so that the unruly might be corrected, it is necessary that there be kings and that they have a scepter, that is, the power to punish their subjects (Proverbs 22:15 says, *Folly is bound close to the heart of a child, but the rod of discipline will drive it far from him,* and Micah 7:14 says, *Shepherd your people with your staff*).

Christ as king also has a scepter to restrain his enemies (in Psalm 2:8-9 God says to the Messiah, *Only ask it of me and I will make your inheritance the nations, your possessions the ends of the earth. With an iron rod you shall shepherd them, like a clay pot you will shatter them*). The psalmist goes on to say that the scepter of your kingdom is a *scepter for justice* to lead the people along the right way. The purpose of law and government is not to flay the people but to make them virtuous. This is the true purpose of politics, and this is something that is worthy of Christ (Psalm 25:5 says, *Guide me in your truth and teach me, for you are God my savior*).

Christ's guidance consists in this: that human beings forsake what is evil and cling to what is good (Isaiah 30:21 says, *"This is the way; walk in it," when you would turn to the right or to the left,* that is, sinning neither by excess nor by defect). This is why the psalmist in verse 8a says, *You love justice and hate wrongdoing.* If a king does not love justice, he will not lead others to what is good, but Christ did so supremely, because, as it says in Psalm 11:7, *The Lord is just and loves just deeds; the upright shall see his face.* Furthermore, if rulers do not hate injustice, they will not punish it, but because Christ hates injustice above all, he punishes those who do evil.

In verse 8b the psalmist says to Christ, *Therefore God, your God has anointed you,* to indicate either the final or the efficient cause of this anointing. In other words, you have acted justly so that God can justly anoint you. Did Christ merit this anointing? Not really, since by reason of his divinity he already possessed it from eternity, but he did merit the revelation of this eternal anointing, and in scripture a thing is often said to happen when it becomes known. By his passion, Christ merited his exaltation in the faith of all peoples. In this sense *therefore* indicates the final cause or purpose of this anointing.

But if *therefore* indicates the efficient cause, then the sense is as follows: So that you might be invested with your throne and your scepter, it is God who has anointed you. In the Old Testament, both priests and kings were anointed. This is evident in the case of David (1 Sm 13:16) and of Solomon (1 Kgs 1:39). Prophets were also anointed, as is evident in the case of Elisha, who received a double portion of Elijah's spirit (2 Kgs 2:9-10). These titles also belong to Christ, since he was a king (Gabriel says to Mary in Luke 1:32, *He shall reign over the house of Jacob forever*); and a priest, who offered himself to God in sacrifice (as it says in Ephesians 5:2, *Christ loved us and handed himself over for us as a sacrificial offering to God for a fragrant aroma*); and a prophet, who announced beforehand the way to salvation (Moses says in Deuteronomy 18:15, *A prophet like me will the Lord, your God, raise up for you from your own kinsmen; to him you shall listen*).

But how was Christ anointed? Not with an oil that was visible, for he declared to Pilate in John 18:36, *My kingdom does not belong to this world*. Furthermore, since he exercised a priesthood which was not material, he was anointed not with material oil but with the oil of the Holy Spirit. This is why the psalmist says, *with the oil of gladness.*

The Holy Spirit is called *oil* for five reasons: First, because just as oil rises above all other liquids, so also the Holy Spirit is above all created beings (Genesis 1:2 says, *A mighty wind moved over the waters*). In other words, the Holy Spirit should be above all things in human hearts, because he is the love of God. Second, because of the Holy Spirit's sweetness, for mercy and all sweetness of mind is from him (as 2 Corinthians 6:6, Latin, says, *. . . in patience, in sweetness, in the Holy Spirit*). A third reason is because oil diffuses itself; in a similar way, the Holy Spirit communicates himself (as 2 Corinthians 13:13 says, *The fellowship of the Holy Spirit be with all of you*, and Romans 5:5 says, *The love of God has been poured out in* *our hearts through the Holy Spirit).* A fourth reason is that oil is fuel for fire and heat, and the Holy Spirit warms and feeds the warmth of love in us (Song of Songs 8:6 says of love, *Its flames are a blazing fire).* Fifth and finally, oil also gives light, and so does the Holy Spirit (Job 32:8 says, *But it is a spirit in man, the breath of the Almighty, that gives him understanding).*

The psalmist says, *Therefore God, your God.* In Latin this particular form of the word for "God" could be either in the nominative or in the vocative case, so there could be a doubt about which it is. But in Greek this is not true because the nominative case takes one form and the vocative another. In the Greek Bible it says, *O God, your God has anointed you with the oil of gladness,* and it gives the sense that the psalmist is addressing Christ, who is God.

Now insofar as Christ is God he cannot be anointed, because he cannot be promoted to a higher status. Therefore, one has to understand that there is something in Christ in terms of which he can be anointed. This "something" is his human nature. Insofar as he is human, he does have a God to anoint him. The psalmist says *the oil of gladness,* because in times of gladness the peoples of the Near East used to anoint themselves with oil (as in Isaiah 61:3 we read, *The spirit of the Lord is upon me, because the Lord has anointed me; he has sent me to bring glad tidings to the lowly, to heal the brokenhearted . . . to give them oil of gladness in place of mourning).*

The Holy Spirit is the cause of joy (Romans 14:17 speaks of *joy in the Holy Spirit,* and Galatians 5:22 of *love, joy, peace,* etc.) It is not possible for the Holy Spirit to be in us without our being glad about the good we have and about our hope for the good to come. The psalmist then says *above your fellow kings,* because Christ was anointed above all other saints (John 1:14 says, *We saw his glory, the glory of the Father's only son, full of grace and truth).* His fellow kings are said to be anointed, yet whatever they have of this oil, the grace of the Holy Spirit, they have as an overflow from Christ (John 1:16 says, *Of his fullness we have all received,* and Psalm 133:2 says, *Like precious ointment on the head, running down upon the beard, upon the beard of Aaron, upon the collar of his robe).*

In verse 9, the psalmist treats of the king's pleasures in respect to four things: his clothing, his dwelling and, in verse 10, his attendants, and his marriage. With regard to the first he says, *With myrrh, aloes, and cassia your robes are fragrant.* The garments of Christ can be understood in two ways: It may refer to his human body (as Isaiah 63:2 asks in reference to Christ's passion, *Why is your apparel red, and your garments like that of the wine presser?*), or it may refer to the Church, Christ's mystical body (Isaiah 49:18 speaking to Zion says of the Israelites returning from exile, *Look about and see, they are all gathering and coming to you. As I live, says the Lord, you shall be arrayed with them all as with adornments, like a bride you shall fasten them on you*).

The fragrance of myrrh and aloes and cassia breathes from these garments, either from the clothing which is Christ's body, or from the Church of the saints. Myrrh has a certain pungency or bitterness, so if it refers to the body of Christ, it indicates the bitterness of his passion (as Song of Songs 5:13, Latin, says, *His fingers* nailed to the cross *are full of the choicest myrrh*). But if it refers to the Church, it symbolizes penance (as Sirach 24:15 says, *Like cinnamon, or fragrant balm, or precious myrrh, I give forth perfume*).

Where our Latin text has *gutta*, the Greek text has *aloes*, and the Hebrew has *stactes*. This is a liquid from a certain plant which is spicy and effective against flatulence and hence signifies humility. This humility was Christ's above all (as he says of himself, Matthew 11:29, *Learn from me, for I am meek and humble of heart*), but it is also to be found in the saints (as Isaiah 66:2 says, *This is the one whom I approve: the lowly and afflicted man who trembles at my word*). Although *aloes* commonly refers to the juice of an herb, here it means a certain tree which is called *aloes* because of its fragrance. *Stactes* is a gum made from myrrh, which is more pleasing than myrrh but of similar fragrance. *Cassia* is of three kinds. One kind of *cassia* is a reed; another is the fruit of a tree, but this is not what is meant here since it is not aromatic. But there is a certain *cassia* which is an aromatic twig, and this is what is being referred to here. Or, according to the *Gloss*, it is a certain tree with an aromatic bark which grows in watery places and thus signifies the water of tears or the water of baptism. In other words, the fragrance of all these things comes forth from the saints and from Christ's body (as 2 Corinthians 2:15 says, *We are the aroma of Christ for God among those who are being saved and among those who are perishing*).

In verse 9, *From ivory-paneled palaces stringed instruments bring you joy*, the psalmist speaks of the king's second pleasure: his palace, that is, the fragrance also comes from your houses of ivory, which is redolent with these perfumes. Among the ancients, walls were of wood, whereas with us they are marble; yet among the Jews and other peoples of the Near East, walls were veneered with ivory (Amos 3:15b says, *The ivory apartments shall be ruined, and their many rooms shall be no more, says the Lord*).

A house symbolizes the Church (as 1 Peter 2:5 says, *Like living stones, let yourselves be built into a spiritual house to be a holy priesthood to offer spiritual sacrifices acceptable to God through Jesus Christ*). The Church is *of ivory*, because it is cool on account of chastity (Song of Songs 5:14 says, *His body is a work of ivory covered with sapphires*), white because of purity, and ruddy because of chastity (Lamentations 4:7 says of the princes of Jerusalem, *Brighter than snow were her princes, whiter than milk, more ruddy than coral, more precious than sapphire*).*

The king's third pleasure is in his attendants, verse 10, *Daughters of kings are your lovely wives* [or as the Latin text reads,] *Because of these things, the daughters of kings have delighted you in your honor*, that is, it is delightful for the daughters of kings to be in the king's service, as if to say, "It is the daughters of kings who serve you by preparing your garments," or literally, "The daughters of earthly kings delight us to the honor of Christ," because they have dedicated themselves to Christ and died for him, as the phrase *in your honor*, that is, *to your honor*, implies, for it is to Christ's honor that the daughters not just of one but of many kings serve him. To interpret this another way: The kings are apostles, and their daughters are faithful souls. Or else, the kings are the teachers of the faith (as Revelation 5:10 says, *You have made them a kingdom and priests*

---

* The Latin unfortunately omits the phrase, *Stringed instruments bring you joy*, so that Thomas could not comment on it.

for our God). Their daughters are the Christian and faithful people (as 1 Corinthians 4:15 says, *I became your father in Christ Jesus through the gospel*). These are daughters in honor of Christ—not in honor of the kings, for example, Peter and Paul, but Christ (1 Corinthians 1:23 says, *We proclaim Christ crucified*), and they are delighted by the perfume of his garments.

The Praise of the Bride, the Church (Mary)

The symbolism of the people of God as Yahweh's bride is found in many of the prophets (for example, Hosea 1-3; Isaiah 1:21-26; Jeremiah 2:22, 3:1, 6-12; Ezekiel 16 and 23), according to some exegetes in The Song of Songs and certainly in Ephesians 5:21-33 and Revelations 21:2, and was applied by Jesus to himself and his Church in certain parables (Mark 2:19-20; Matthew 9:15, 25:1-13; Luke 5:34-35; John 3:29). It is the privileged metaphor to express the mutuality of the covenant of faithful love between God and his chosen people. The Blessed Virgin Mary, as the type of the faithful Church, is also symbolized by the bride, and this applies to every faithful Christian. The great mystics have found no better way to express the mystical union than to speak of it as the "Spiritual Marriage."

The psalmist, in verse 10b, begins to speak of the king's bride and says, *A princess arrayed in Ophir's gold comes to stand at your right hand*. The psalmist has already praised Christ on account of his graciousness, his military skill and his royal pleasures; now he also praises him on account of his bride. He describes her in four ways: in terms of the bride's presence, her dignity, her glory, and her adornment.

The bride of Christ is the Church; the bride of a king is called a queen (King Ahasuerus in Esther 2:17 *placed the royal diadem on her head and made her queen*). Thus, the Church is this queen (2 Corinthians 11:2 says, *I betrothed you to one husband as a chaste virgin to Christ*). Her dignity is the fact that she is queen. She has stood at God's side, always cleaving to him and united to him. So also the angels who are not sent out are called those who stand by God's side (Daniel 7:10 tells of the *thousands upon thousands* of such angels who were *ministering to him, and myriads upon myriads* who *attended him*, and Psalm 5:4 says, *At dawn you will hear my cry; at dawn I will plead before you and wait*). Gregory the Great says of the Church, "She sees, indeed, by faith; she is lifted up by hope; she is united by love."

The glory of this queen is the prerogative she has; she is *at your right hand*, meaning, she shares in the better goods of the king. Similarly, insofar as he shares in the Father's better goods, the Son as a human being is said to sit at the right hand of the Father (as Mark 16:19 says, *So then the Lord Jesus, after he spoke to them, was taken up into heaven and took his seat at the right hand of the Father*), and this implies better things, for if spiritual things are compared with temporal things, the spiritual are the better. This queen has stood amidst spiritual goods (Proverbs 3:16 says of wisdom, *Long life is in her right hand, in her left are riches and honor*). Furthermore, if the right hand signifies good works, these are certainly better than sins (Proverbs 4:27, Latin, says, *The Lord knows the ways that are on his right*), and in the midst of such goodness stands the queen.

Her adornment is described when the psalmist says *arrayed in Ophir's gold*. Neither the version of Jerome nor the Hebrew has the phrase found in the Latin *surrounded with variety*. What Jerome does have is *in a golden diadem*. The Hebrew text has *in a quantity of gold*.* According to our Latin text, there are two aspects to the Church's clothing. The first is the teaching of the Old and New Testaments (Proverbs 31:21 says, *All her charges are doubly clothed*). This clothing is not solid gold but is threaded with gold; it shines with divine wisdom because her teaching is filled with it.

Furthermore, it is *surrounded with variety*. This can refer either to different kinds of languages or to a deeper sort of wisdom. In another sense, her clothing is virtuous activity (Psalm 132:16 says, *I will clothe her priests with blessing*). Now gold symbolizes love (Genesis 2:12 says, *The gold of that land is the best*). Since love is

---

* *Ophir's gold* was not in the texts known to Thomas, but see 1 Kings 9:28, 10:11; Job 22:24.

thought of as radiant and rosy, her clothing is called golden, because it takes its color from love (as 1 Corinthians 16:14 says, *Your every act should be done in love*). Her clothing is also *surrounded with variety*, that is, with deeds of the different virtues. Some deeds are golden by reason of martyrdom; others are purple by reason of penitential sighing (Colossians 3:12 says, *Put on, God's chosen ones, holy and beloved, heartfelt compassion, kindness, humility, gentleness, and patience*).

All of this can also be interpreted in terms of the Blessed Virgin, who is the queen and mother of the King. She stands above all the choirs of heaven in clothing that is threaded with gold, with divinity—not that she is God, but because she is the mother of God.

In verse 11 we read, *Listen, my daughter, and understand; pay me careful heed*. Then the bride is praised for four reasons: for her beauty in verses 11-13; for the excellence of her glory in verse 14-15a; for her companions in verses 15b-16; and in verses 17-18 for her offspring. With regard to the first of these, the psalmist makes two observations: First, he sets forth how she acquires her beauty or graciousness; then, in verse 12, he describes her graciousness.

Thus, he first renders her attentive by saying, *Listen, my daughter*. He calls the Church that is to come a daughter for two reasons. One reason is that David, the psalmist, is speaking in his own person. Now insofar as we cling to Christ, the son of Abraham, we too are sons and daughters of Abraham, and since Christ is the son of David, we are also sons and daughters of David. The other reason is that he is speaking in the person of the apostles; they have generated us in Christ Jesus through the gospel. This is why he says *Listen, my daughter* (as James 1:19 says, *Everyone should be quick to hear, slow to speak*, that is, to hear the gospel or Christ's word, and Luke 11:28 says, *Blessed are they who hear the word of God and observe it*).

Or else the psalmist is referring to the writings of the prophets: Listen to them in order to believe in Christ (as Isaiah 53:1 asks, *Who would believe what we have heard?*). *Listen . . . and understand*—here we understand by faith, but in the future we will see by vision (1 Corinthians 13:12 says, *At present we see indistinctly, as in a mirror, then face to face*). Or else it means to understand that Christ has been born one of us (as it is said of wisdom in Baruch 3:38, *Since then she [wisdom] has appeared on earth and moved among men*, and John 1:14 says, *And we saw his glory, the glory of the Father's only son, full of grace and truth*). *Pay me careful heed*, by way of humility, so that you might obey (as Sirach 6:33 says, *If you are willing to listen, you will learn; if you give heed, you will be wise*).

In verse 11, *Forget your people and your father's house*, the psalmist gives this figurative advice because the queen comes to David or Solomon from an alien people. She is, therefore, admonished lest she keep thinking of her own family. This fits the Church, because she is called to Christ from an alien people, either from the unbelieving Jews or from the unbelieving Gentiles, and, as Augustine says, "No one can come to the new life in Christ unless he repents of his old life," that is, of sin.

This is why the psalmist says, *Forget your people* (1 Chronicles 16:20 says of the Jews, *Wandering from nation to nation, from one kingdom to another people*) *and your father's house*, that is, Satan's house (as Jesus says to those who claimed to be saved, simply because they were children of Abraham in John 8:44, *You belong to your father the devil and you willingly carry out your father's desires*, and God in Ezekiel 16:3 says of faithless Israel, *Your father was an Amorite*). Or else, it is the house of sin or of carnal desires (as Joseph says in Genesis 41:51, *God has made me forget the sufferings I endured at the hands of my family*). This is symbolized by the captive girl of Deuteronomy 21:12-13, who is commanded to shave her head and mourn her father and mother as if they were dead, before she can be married by a Jewish husband.

Next, in verse 12, we read *that the king might desire your beauty*. Here the psalmist promises the bride the king's favor. First, she will gain the king's love; then, in verse 13b, she will gain the people's favor, that is, honor. Hence, he promises the king's love and shows her the king's dignity. He says: "If you forget your people and your father's house, you will acquire thereby a spiritual beauty" (as Psalm 26:8 says, *Lord, I love the house where you dwell, the tenting-place of your glory*). This beauty is greatly desirable to her spiritual bridegroom; this is why the psalmist says *that the king might desire your beauty.* This beauty is the beauty of justice (as Jeremiah 31:23, Latin, says, *May the Lord bless you, O beauty of justice*).

He might *desire* means that the king will take delight in you (as Isaiah 62:4 says, *No more shall men call you "Forsaken," or your land "Desolate," but you shall be called "My Delight," and your land "Espoused"*). This is something to be desired, because this king is great in authority, in nature, and in honor: Verse 13, *honor him, daughter of Tyre.* He should be honored, first, because he is king and therefore Lord (as Psalm 100:3 says, *Know that the Lord is God*); second, because he is God (as Psalm 95:3 says, *For the Lord is the great God*); and third, because all the peoples of the world, even the most remote, worship him (as Psalm 86:9 says, *All the nations you have made shall come to bow before you, Lord, and give honor to your name,* and Zephaniah 2:11b says, *Then, each from its own place, all the coastlands of the nations shall adore him*).

Those nearby will also worship him, since it says *daughters of Tyre* will come with gifts,* and Tyre is close to the Promised Land. Thus, the *daughters,* that is, the inhabitants of that land, *will entreat your favor;* in other words, they will subject themselves to you with gifts. This was fulfilled when the Canaanite woman left the borders of Tyre and came to Jesus (see Matthew 15); or else,** *Then the richest of the people will seek your favor with gifts,* that is, the people who are in Tyre, *will seek your favor with gifts.*

The name *Tyre* can also be interpreted as "distress," and thus all who are in distress will seek your favor. Indeed, literally, all the distressed did come to Jesus (Luke 4:40 says, *At sunset, all who had people sick with various diseases brought them to him. He laid his hands on each of them and cured them,* and Isaiah 26:16 says, *O Lord, oppressed by your punishment, we cried out in anguish under your chastising. . . . But your dead shall live, their corpses shall rise; awake and sing, you who lie in the dust*). And those who are saved offer gifts, that is, they offer themselves—or else, alms (Isaiah 19:21

---

* NAB has the singular, "daughter," and refers it to the queen.
** According to the reading favored by the NAB.

predicts of the pagan Egyptians, *They offer sacrifices and oblations, and fulfill the vows they made to the Lord*).

The psalmist has just praised the bride for her beauty; now, in verse 14, he praises her for her glory, both inner and outer. He deals with inner glory when he says, *All glorious is the king's daughter as she enters*, that is, within the king's dwelling. This interior glory is verified in three ways. First, her glory is in her inner conscience and not in outward fame from human beings, as is the fame of sinners (2 Corinthians 1:12 says, *For our boast is this, the testimony of our conscience that we have conducted ourselves in the world, and especially toward you, with the simplicity and sincerity of God, and not by human wisdom but by the grace of God*).

Second, in interior justice, not in exterior observance, as in the Old Testament it was sometimes thought to be (as Romans 2:29 says, *One is not a Jew outwardly. True circumcision is not outward as in the flesh. Rather, one is a Jew inwardly, and circumcision is of the heart, in the spirit, not the letter; his praise is not from human beings but from God*).

Third, it involves a hope which is eternal (something inward) and not a hope for things of time (something external) (as Jesus says in Matthew 6:1, *Take care not to perform righteous deeds in order that people may see them; otherwise, you will have no recompense from your heavenly Father*).

The psalmist, however, also speaks of an exterior glory when he says, *her raiment threaded with gold*. This raiment means the teaching of the Church (in Exodus 28:33-35 God orders that on the hem of the priest's vestment there should be bells, whose sound can be heard by all. The sound symbolizes his teaching). Thus, in the teaching of divine wisdom, which is symbolized by gold, there is great glory. But in verse 15 it is said of the queen that *In embroidered apparel she is led to the king*, that is, she is embellished and adorned by many languages, namely, the various modes of teaching, which, however, all speak the same truth (Acts of the Apostles 2:4 says that the apostles *were all filled with the Holy Spirit and began to speak in different tongues, as the Spirit enabled them to proclaim*).

Or else, *embroidered* refers to inner purity and the ornamentation of the virtues, while *apparel* refers to external appearance. In other words, all her glory is from within, and these two things, purity and the virtues, are to be found principally in the golden embroidery. By this metaphor one can also understand the goal of life, either for the whole Church or for the whole human person. In clothing the embroidered border is often the hem of the garment, and the text does not say it is merely the color of gold, but that it is *threaded with gold*. The *Gloss* says that it is those who have become perfected and holy who will be seen as gold at the end of the world.

Moreover, as long as persons are making progress they are, as it were, of gold color, but when they reach their goal, they will be truly gold, perfect in splendor (Proverbs 4:18 says, *The path of the just is like a shining light that grows in brilliance until perfect day*). Thus, when the psalmist says the bride is arrayed in *embroidered apparel*, this means she is adorned with a variety of nations or a variety of graces and virtues.

In verse 15b, when it says, *The maids of her train are presented to the king*, the queen is praised because of her companions, and in this regard the psalmist makes three observations. First, he describes her companions; then, in verse 16a, how they attain to her company; and finally in 16b where this company is headed. . . .*

Two groups of attendants seem mentioned, the *maids* of verse 15, and the *they* of verse 16. If they are taken to be one and the same, then this is the meaning: Virgins, that is, faithful souls who are not corrupted by sin, are led inside to the king, that is, to Christ, who is the King of kings. It is said *presented to the king*, because they do not come of themselves (Jesus in John 6:44 says, *No one comes to me unless the Father who sent me draws him*, and this is why in Song of Songs 1:4 the bride says, *Draw me! . . . Bring me, O king, to your chambers!*). But they are led in with the queen, that is, with the universal Church, because no one comes nor is led in to Christ unless that one follows the teachings of the Church.

Or else, they are led in with the Blessed Virgin, because Christ's

---

* Thomas then reports the version of Jerome and the Hebrew, which are followed by the NAB as above.

virgins are led to him in order to preserve chastity and to exercise the other virtues. The others are neighbors of hers, namely, of the Church or of the Blessed Virgin; they are *presented to the king*. With regard to the virgins, the psalmist says that they are *presented*, because they are converted to Christ more easily, but with regard to the other attendants he says that they are *led in*, because they are drawn in with more difficulty (2 Timothy 4:2 says, *Proclaim the word; be persistent whether it is convenient or inconvenient*, that is, whether it is easily accepted or not).

If *maids* and *they* are understood to be different groups, then the *maids* means those who have been made perfect; these are described as if they want to go of their own volition (as Psalm 105:43 says, *He brought his people out with joy, his chosen ones with shouts of triumph*), that is, they are brought in with interior joy and exterior triumph, for they have willingly offered themselves to Christ (as Psalm 54:8 says, *Then I will offer you generous sacrifice and praise your gracious name*). Or else, they are brought into heaven by the angels (in the parable of the rich man and Lazarus Jesus recounts in Luke 16:22 how *when the poor man died, he was carried to the bosom of Abraham*).

To where is the procession brought? Into the palace (Latin, "temple") of the king, verse 16. By the fact that he uses the word *temple*, it is clear the psalmist is speaking about the king who is Christ and God, that is, that they themselves might be a temple for the king (1 Corinthians 3:17 says, *The temple of God, which you are, is holy*). Or else, so they might contemplate in the temple of God, that is, be free to attend to God, since that is the very purpose of a community of virgins (1 Corinthians 7:14 says, *An unmarried woman or a virgin is anxious about the things of the Lord, so that she may be holy in both body and spirit. A married woman, on the other hand, is anxious about the things of the world, how she may please her husband*).

The Apostles

Thomas had a special reverence for the Apostles, as appears in many references to them, since he believed that no one would ever exceed them in spiritual gifts (except, of course, Christ's Mother) (*Summa Theologiae*, I-II, q. 106, 4 c.). His spirituality is ecclesial in the highest degree, because for him Christian holiness comes from incorporation in Christ, and the Body of Christ is the Church, the community of faith, hope and love. Hence, his emphasis on Christ's continued presence in the Church, not only in the eucharist but also through the Petrine office of chief shepherd in the Church, an office necessary to its unity and vitality (*Summa Theologiae*, II-II, q. 1, a.10).

Finally, in verses 17-18, the psalmist praises the queen for her offspring, mentioning four things about them: their origin, dignity, office and fruit. He says first in verse 17a, *The throne of your fathers your sons will have.* The sons of the primitive Church are the apostles and their successors. Some are called sons, because they are born to the Church through the teaching of Christ, her husband; others are born through the teaching of the apostles, and still others are sons of other preachers. Thus it is not inappropriate to say that the same men are both *sons* and *fathers*.

The apostles themselves were *fathers* of those whom they converted (as 1 Corinthians 4:15 says, *Even if you should have countless guides to Christ, yet you do not have many fathers, for I became your father in Christ Jesus through the gospel*). Others also were both *fathers* and *sons*. All of these are sons who have been born to the Church: sons of the apostles and of other holy men and teachers. Or else, the good *fathers* were the prophets (Sirach 44:1 says, *Now will I praise those godly men, our ancestors, each in his own time*). In place of those prophets, sons have been born to the Church who exercise their dignity, the prophetic office.

Thus, who are the offspring of the bride and their origin are clear; now follows in verse 17b the mention of their dignity: *You shall make them princes through all the land,* that is, those who are first to claim land, claim what is the best land; hence, they are called princes,* because they first received the gifts of the Holy Spirit and in their plenitude (Romans 8:23 says, *We ourselves, who have the firstfruits of the Spirit*). The *Gloss* says that the first Christians received the Spirit more abundantly than we who have come later. Just as no other woman can be compared to the Blessed Virgin, so no other saint can be compared or treated as an equal to the apostles.

They are also called princes, because they were and still are the rulers of the churches, and also because they were, after Christ, our first teachers (Psalm 68:26 says, *Your procession comes in view, O God, your procession into the holy place, my God and king, the singers* [Latin: *princes*] *go first*, etc., and as Deborah and Barak in Judges 5:9 sang, these princes should be loved: *My heart is with the leaders of Israel, nobles of the people who bless the Lord*). *You shall make them princes*, for they are chosen by Christ not by themselves (as Jesus says in John 15:16, *It is not you who chose me, but I who chose you and appointed you to go and bear fruit that will remain, so that whatever you ask the Father in my name he may give you*).

Furthermore, other bishops are established by the Supreme Pontiff, the pope (Hebrews 5:4 says, *No one takes this honor upon himself, but only when called by God as Aaron was*). And this is not just in a certain land or time, but verse 18 says, *I will make your name renowned through all generations; thus nations shall praise you forever* (Psalm 19:5 says, *Yet their report goes forth through all the earth, their message to the ends of the world*, and Psalm 20:7, *Now I know victory is given to the anointed of the Lord*).

All this is especially true of Peter and Paul: Peter received universal sovereignty over the Church (Jesus in John 21:17 says to Peter, *Feed my sheep*) and Paul received a mission to all the Gentile nations (Paul in Acts of the Apostles 13:47 cites Isaiah 49:6, *I have made you a light to the Gentiles, that you may be an instrument of salvation to the ends of the earth*).

In verse 18a, the psalmist with the words *I will make your name renowned through all generations* now describes the apostles' office,

---

* Latin for "first men."

which is to preach the name of God (Jesus in Mark 16:15 says, *Go into the whole world and proclaim the gospel to every creature*). Then when the psalmist says, *I will make your name renowned through all the nations*, he means the apostles will make others remember everywhere and for all time the name of God (as Jesus in Mark 13:31 says, *Heaven and earth will pass away but my words will not pass away*, and in Matthew 28:20 says, *Behold, I am with you always, until the end of the age*).

Finally, in verse 19b, the psalmist says, *Thus nations shall praise you forever*, and with this presents the fruit of the apostles' labors, which is that all peoples will acknowledge Christ. He says *nations*, because not just one people but all are included (as Psalm 67:4 says, *May the peoples praise you, O God! May all the peoples praise you!* and Philippians 2:11 says, *And every tongue confess that Jesus Christ is Lord to the glory of God the Father*). While the Latin has *forever and for age upon age*, these expressions are equivalent to the Greek for *eternity* (as Isaiah 35:10 says, *Those whom the Lord has ransomed will return and enter Zion singing, crowned with everlasting joy; They will meet with joy and gladness, sorrow and mourning will flee*); but according to the *Gloss*, *forever* means in the present age, and *for age upon age* means in the future.

Although the Latin reads *They will remember your name, O Lord*, the reading *I will make your name renowned* is better, and it refers to the fruits of the apostles' preaching and is said in the name of the people who have been converted. In other words, I am saying that you will establish them as princes and I, the Christian people, will remember your name forever. This points to faith, which is in the heart, and afterward praise, which comes from faith.

This psalm is sung on the Feast of the Lord's Nativity because of the praise of the bridegroom, the king, in its first part; and on the feasts of the Blessed Virgin, the queen, whose praises are in its second part. It is also sung on the feasts of virgins, because they are the queen's attendants and on feasts of apostles because of verse 17, *The throne of your fathers your sons will have; you shall make them princes through all the land.*

A Eucharistic Hymn

At Urban IV's request, Thomas composed the liturgical texts for the Feast of Corpus Christi. The authenticity of the beautiful hymn *Adoro te devote*, related to this liturgy and still used to today in the rite of Benediction of the Blessed Sacrament, has been questioned but also ably defended. It is profoundly theological, yet also very medieval in its reference to Christ as the mother Pelican who, according to legend, fed its young on its own blood by piercing its breast with its beak. We conclude with a deeply felt translation of this hymn by the great Jesuit poet Gerald Manley Hopkins, to illustrate Thomas' great devotion to the eucharist and the central place it occupies in his spirituality as the supreme sacrament, in which the Incarnate Word remains present in his Church, its source of life and unity.

As Thomas is reported to have said that he learned more from his crucifix than from books, it is also related that when he was especially puzzled by a theological problem he used to lean his aching head against the tabernacle, praying for enlightenment.

The Poetical Works of Gerald Manley Hopkins, edited by Norman H. McKenzie (Oxford: Clarendon Press, 1992), no. 100, gives three versions of this poem and an incomplete fourth version. Our text is version (b), p. 112, but with the revisions in the incomplete version (d), pp. 113 f.

Adoro Te Devote

I bow down before thee, Godhead hiding here
Under only shadows, shapes that but appear:
Lord, all at thy service low there lies a heart
Lost, all lost in wonder at the God thou art.

Seeing, touching, tasting are in thee deceived;
How the trusty hearing? that may be believed:
What God's Son has told me, take for truth I do;
Truth himself speaks truly or there's nothing true.

On the cross thy godhead made no sign to men;
Here thy very manhood keeps from mortal ken:
Both are my confession, both are my belief,
And I pray the prayer of the dying thief.

I am not like Thomas, wounds I cannot see,
But can plainly call thee Lord and God as he:
This faith each day deeper be my holding of,
Daily make me harder hope and dearer love.

O thou our reminder of Christ crucified,
Living Bread the life of us for whom he died,
Lend this life to me then: feed and feast my mind,
There be Thou the sweetness man was meant to find.

Bring the tender tale true of the Pelican;
Bathe me, Jesu Lord, in what thy bosom ran—
Blood that but one drop of has the world to win
All the world forgiveness of its world of sin.

Jesu whom I look at veilèd here below,
I beseech thee send me what I thirst for so,
Some day to gaze on thee face to face in light
And be blest for ever with thy glory's sight.
Amen.

Chronology

(Based on James A. Weisheipl, *Friar Thomas D'Aquino*, New York, 1974. The authenticity of prayers, sermons, the letter *De modo studendi*, and some short works on logic and natural philosophy is still uncertain).

1224 Thomas is born at Roccasecca, near the Benedictine Abbey of Monte Cassino, in the Kingdom of Sicily, son of Count Landulf d'Aquino and his second wife Theodora. He had two half-brothers, four brothers and five sisters.

1230 Dedicated to the Abbey and there educated.

1239 Sent by the abbott to study liberal arts at the University of Naples.

1243 Death of his father.

1244 He took the habit of the Order of Preachers but was abducted by his brothers and retained at home with his mother for almost a year; may have written two short works on logic at this time.

1245 Went to Paris for novitiate and study under Albert the Great.

1248 At Cologne with Albert the Great.

1250 Ordained priest at Cologne; he may have written his commentaries on *Jeremiah* and *Lamentations* this early.

1252 Teaching at the University of Paris he wrote *De ente et essentia* and his first major work, the *Commentary on the Sentences of Peter Lombard*, perhaps also commented *Isaiah* 1-11.

1256 Became Regent Master in Theology at Paris, after attacks by secular faculty against right of mendicants to teach was settled in favor of the friars by the intervention of Pope Alexander IV. Wrote two inaugural sermons commending sacred scripture, his *Contra impugnantes Dei cultum et religionem* against William St. Amour, the disputed questions *De Veritate,* Quodlibeta 7-11, the *Commentary on Matthew,* the *Commentaries on Boethius' De Trinitate and De Hebdomadibus.*

1259   Attended a general chapter of his order in Valenciennes, to help design the program of studies for Dominicans, returned briefly to Paris, began his second major work, the *Summa Contra Gentiles,* and perhaps the *Compendium theologiae,* and then went to Naples in his own Dominican province to teach.

1261   Taught at the court of Pope Urban IV at Orvieto until the pope died in 1264. Here Thomas wrote the *Corpus Christi* liturgy and completed the *Summa Contra Gentiles,* as well as the *Commentary on Job* and the *Catena Aurea* of the gospels and the *Contra errores Graecorum.*

1265   Assigned by order to open a house of studies in Rome, he wrote disputed questions *De Potentia* and *De Malo,* maybe the *Commentary on Dionysius' De divinis nominibus* and responses and letters to many inquiries from bishops, the King of Cyprus and others on current theological and ethical problems.

1267   Began his masterpiece, the *Summa Theologiae.*

1268   Assigned to court of Pope Clement IV in Viterbo he probably wrote *De spiritualibus creaturis* and finished the First Part of the *Summa Theologiae,* but in two months returned to Paris as Regent Master to meet the renewed attacks on the friars in the University by Gerard of Abbeville against whom he wrote *Contra doctrinam retrahentium a religione.*

1269   Aquinas taught as Regent Master at University of Paris for the second time and wrote the whole Second Part of the *Summa Theologiae,* probably the rest of the *Quaestiones Disputatae* and the *Quodlibeta,* the commentaries on *John* and the *Epistles of Paul.* He became involved in the controversy between the Faculties of Theology and of Liberal Arts over the latter's Averroistic Aristotelianism and defended his own use of Aristotle by writing *De unitate intellectus contra Averroistas, De aeternitate mundi contra murmurantes,* and many of his commentaries on Aristotle. He also wrote responses to many inquiries on current theological topics.

1270   The first condemnation of Averroism by the Archbishop of Paris.

1272   Thomas left Paris, went briefly to Florence, then home to Naples where he wrote the Third Part of the *Summa Theologiae,* the *Commentary on the Psalms,* the rest of his Aristotle commentaries and the sermons on the creed, Our Father, Ten Commandments, and Hail Mary.

1273 On December 6 he ceased to write, leaving the *Summa Theologiae* incomplete as to the sacraments of penance, anointing of the sick, matrimony, orders, and eschatology, to be supplemented by disciples from his other writings.

1274 In February he set out for the Council of Lyons, suffered a head injury on the journey, was nursed by his niece at the castle of Maenza, then was carried to the Cistercian Monastery of Fossonova, where he died on March 7.

1277 Averroism condemned by Stephen Tempier, Archbishop of Paris, and Archbishop Robert Kilwardby, O.P., at Oxford. Aquinas was not named, but some of his teaching seemed implicated.

1323 Canonized St. Thomas Aquinas by John XXII.

1325 Revocation of Paris condemnation as regards Aquinas' teaching.

1567 Made Doctor of the Church.

1879 Encyclical *Aeterni Patris* commending him as *Doctor Communis* of the Church and his philosophy and theology as basis of Catholic education.

1965 Vatican II in its "Decree on Priestly Formation" (*Optatus Totius*) commends him as the guide for future priests in study of systematic theology.

A Select Bibliography

Arintero, Juan G. *The Mystical Evolution in the Development and Vitality of the Church*, 2 vols. St. Louis: B. Herder Book Co., 1949; a systematic Thomistic treatise on the spiritual life.

Ashley, Benedict M. *The Dominicans*. Religious Order Series, vol. 3. Collegeville: The Liturgical Press/Michael Glazier, 1990; pp. 25-56 deals with Thomas in historical context.

Chenu, M.-D. *St. Thomas d'Aquin et la Théologie*. Maîtres Spirituels, vol. 17. Paris: Cerf, 1959.

_____. *Toward Understanding Saint Thomas Aquinas*. Translated by A.-M. Henry and Dominic Hughes. Chicago: Regnery, 1964; a good introduction to historical background and works of Aquinas.

Farrell, Walter. *A Companion to the Summa*, 4 vols. New York: Sheed and Ward, 1939; a non-technical presentation of Aquinas' theological synthesis.

Fox, Matthew. *Sheer Joy: Conversations with Thomas Aquinas on Creation Spirituality*. Foreword by Rupert Sheldrake. Afterword by Bede Griffiths. San Francisco: Harper-Collins, 1992; an original way of presenting St. Thomas' spirituality in terms of positive, negative, creative, and transformative ways, but "revised" to fit the author's own views.

Gardeil, Antoine. *The Gifts of the Holy Ghost in Dominican Saints*. Milwaukee: Bruce, 1937; an interesting application of the Thomistic view of the gifts of the Holy Spirit to concrete examples, by an important theologian of religious experience.

Garrigou-Lagrange, Reginald. *Christian Perfection and Contemplation*. Translated by Timothea Doyle. St. Louis: B. Herder Book Co., 1939; a defense of the Thomistic view of the universal call to contemplation.

_____. *The Three Ages of the Interior Life: Prelude to Eternal Life*, 2 vols. Translated by Timothea Doyle. St. Louis: B. Herder Book Co., 1948;

a classic treatise on the theology of spiritual life based on Aquinas. A short version is The Three Ways of the Spiritual Life. London: Burns, Oates and Washbourne, 1938.

_____. "The Character and Principles of Dominican Spirituality," in Dominican Spirituality. Edited by Anselm Townsend. Milwaukee: Bruce, 1934, pp. 57-82; an attempt to state Aquinas' principles of spirituality.

Grabmann, Martin. Interior Life of Thomas Aquinas: Presented from His Works and the Acts of his Canonization Process. Translated by Nicholas Ashenbrener. Milwaukee: Bruce, 1951; a noted expert on Aquinas and medieval spirituality.

Hinnebusch, William. Dominican Spirituality: Principles and Practice. Washington: The Thomist Press, 1965, see bibliography, pp. 145-148.

_____. History of the Dominican Order, 2 vols. Staten Island: Alba House, 1966-73; volume 2 of this history, which was completed only to 1500, contains much material on the Dominican writers of this period.

McNabb, Vincent. "The Mysticism of St. Thomas Aquinas," in Thomas Aquinas: Being Papers Read at the Celebrations of the Sixth Centenary of the Canonization of Saint Thomas Aquinas, Manchester, 1924. Edited by Alfred Whitacre, et al. St. Louis: B. Herder Book Co., 1925, pp. 89-109.

Nicholas, Jean-Hervé. Contemplation et Vie Contemplative en Christianisme. Paris: Editions Beauchesne, 1980; a noted Thomist theologian reviews controversies on the nature of contemplation.

Petitot, Hyacinthe. The Life and Spirit of Thomas Aquinas. Translated by Cyprian Burke. Chicago: Priory Press, 1966; a penetrating study of Aquinas' interior life.

Poinsot, Jean (John of St. Thomas). The Gifts of the Holy Ghost. Translated by Dominic Hughes. New York: Sheed and Ward, 1951; a classical theological treatise on Thomas' doctrine of the gifts.

Principe, Walter H. "Thomas Aquinas' Spirituality." The Étienne Gilson Series, no. 7. Toronto: Pontifical Institute of Medieval Studies, 1984.

Royo, Antonio and Jordan Aumann. The Theology of Christian Perfection. Dubuque: Priory Press, 1962; a systematic treatise on spiritual life based on Thomistic principles.

Ruane, Edward. "The Spirituality of the Preacher," in In the Company of Preachers. Aquinas Institute of Theology Faculty. Edited by Edward Ruane. Collegeville: The Liturgical Press, 1993, pp. 151-64; an essay giving Aquinas' background as a preacher.

Tugwell, Simon. The Way of the Preacher. Springfield: Tempelgate, 1979; this and the two following items by Tugwell are very helpful in placing Aquinas' spirituality in historical context.

_____. "The Mendicants," pp. 294-95 and "The Dominicans," pp. 296-300 in *The Study of Spirituality*. Edited by Chesyln Jones, Geoffrey Wainwright, Edward Yarnold. New York: Oxford University Press, 1986.

_____. *Albert and Thomas: Selected Writings*. New York: Paulist Press, 1988.

Walgrave, Valentine. *Dominican Self-Appraisal In the Light of the Council*. Chicago: Priory Press, 1968; a discussion of how Thomistic spirituality can be reconciled with Vatican II developments.

Weisheipl, James A. *Thomas D'Aquino*. Garden City: Doubleday, 1974; the standard life of St. Thomas. "A Brief Catalogue of Authentic Works," pp. 355-406 also lists English translations of works.